Hurlyburly

OTHER PLAYS BY DAVID RABE

The Basic Training of Pavlo Hummel
Sticks and Bones
The Orphan
In the Boom Boom Room
Streamers

Hurlyburly

A Play by DAVID RABE

GROVE PRESS, INC./New York

First Edition 1985
First Printing 1985
ISBN: 0-394-54609-1
Library of Congress Catalog Card Number:

First Evergreen Edition 1985

ISBN: 0-394-62011-9
Library of Congress Catalog Card Number:

Library of Congress Cataloging in Publication Data

Rabe, David.
    Hurlyburly.

    I. Title.
PS3568.A23H8 1985   812'.54   85-770
ISBN 0-394-54609-1
ISBN 0-394-62011-9 (pbk.)

6 5 4 3 2

Manufactured in the United States of America

GROVE PRESS, INC., 196 West Houston Street, New York, N.Y. 10014

For Ellen Neuwald

Hurlyburly was originally produced at the Goodman Theatre, Chicago, Gregory Mosher, Artistic Director, on April 2, 1984, with the following cast:

Eddie	*William Hurt*
Phil	*Harvey Keitel*
Mickey	*Christopher Walken*
Artie	*Jerry Stiller*
Donna	*Cynthia Nixon*
Darlene	*Sigourney Weaver*
Bonnie	*Judith Ivey*

Directed by MIKE NICHOLS

The scenery was by Tony Walton; costumes by Ann Roth; lighting by Jennifer Tipton; sound by Michael Schweppe. The production stage manager was Peter Lawrence.

The New York premiere of the play took place on June 21, 1984 at the Promenade Theatre presented by Icarus Productions and Frederick M. Zollo, with Ivan Bloch and ERB Productions and William P. Suter as Associate Producer. It opened with the same cast and designers as in Chicago and under the direction of Mike Nichols.

Hurlyburly premiered on Broadway in New York at the Ethel Barrymore Theatre on August 7, 1984, again presented by Icarus Productions and Frederick M. Zollo, with Ivan Bloch and ERB Productions and William P. Suter as Associate Producer. The cast and designers were the same as in the two previous presentations, except that the part of Mickey was played by Ron Silver instead of Christopher Walken, and the sound was by Otts Munderloh. The direction was again by Mike Nichols.

CHARACTERS

Eddie   Darlene
Phil   Bonnie
Mickey   Donna
Artie

Hurlyburly

SCENE ONE

TIME: A little while ago.

PLACE: A two-story house crowded into one of the canyons between Sunset Boulevard and Mulholland Drive in the Hollywood Hills.

A spacious living room leading into an open kitchen make up the entire first floor of the house. Steps lead upstairs to an exposed balcony which overlooks the living room. A rail runs along the balcony and stairway. Three doors feed onto the balcony—Eddie's bedroom and Mickey's bedroom, which are separated by a bathroom. Stage right there is a couch and a low coffee table with a portable television on top of it and piles of newspapers and magazines on the couch and the floor around it. Directly upstage and yet slightly off center is the door to the outside. Along this wall there is perhaps a closet door with a mirror inside of it. Slightly right of center stage is an armchair angled toward the couch. A hassock sits beside it. Upstage of the couch is a window seat, the outdoor foliage visible beyond it; books, photos, résumés are scattered on the window seat. At the far stage left is a pile of throw pillows; and if the closet door and mirror are inappropriate along the back wall, perhaps they are in this wall. The kitchen area is a nook, with a counter running out downstage and swivel chairs on either side. Upstage are the stove, refrigerator, cabinets. The nook itself has shelves in which there are liquor bottles, magazines, scripts.

The house is completely surrounded by wild vegetation, which is visible through greenhouse-like windows in the living room and kitchen. At the far right is an old rocking chair. It is worth noting that in the characters' speeches phrases such as "whatchamacallit," "thingamajig," "blah-blah-blah" and "rapateta" abound. These are phrases used by the characters to keep themselves talking and should be said unhesitatingly with the authority and conviction with which one would have in fact said the missing word.

As the curtain rises, Eddie is asleep on the couch. The TV on the coffee table in front of the couch is droning out the early morning news. Eddie is a mess, his shirt out, wrinkled, unbuttoned, his trousers remaining on him only because one leg is yet tangled around one ankle. He lies

13

with his head downstage, and as the door opens and Phil, a muscular, anxious man in a hurry comes rushing in, Eddie instantly sits straight up and appears to be looking right at Phil.

Phil: Eddie.

Eddie: What? *(Eddie flops back onto the couch as if he has just been hit on the head.)*

Phil: Eddie, you awake or not?

Eddie: I don't know. How about you?

Phil: Eddie, I'm standin' here. How you doin'?

Eddie: I don't know. Did I leave the door open?

Phil: It was open.

Eddie *(Sitting up, a man in command, and talking, almost bragging, as he turns off the TV)*: I come home last night, I was feelin' depressed. I sat around, I watched some TV. Somebody called and hung up when I answered. I smoked some dope, took a couple of ludes. The TV got to look very good. It was a bunch of shit, but it looked very good due to the dope and due to the ludes. So I musta fell asleep at some point. *(As nodding a little, it appears he might sleep again.)*

Phil *(Heading for the kitchen)*: Maybe I'll make us some coffee. Where is everything? By the stove and stuff?

Eddie: What time is it?

Phil *(Holding up his left wrist and watch, he yells)*: I can't tell you what time it is: my watch was broken by the blow.

Eddie: There's a clock on the stove.

Phil: It's over.

Eddie: What?

Phil: Everything.

Eddie *(Rising, staggering toward the kitchen, his trousers dragging along by the ankle)*: What EVERYTHING?

Phil: Me and Susie.

Eddie: Whata you mean, "everything"?

Phil: Everything. The whole thing. You know. Our relationship. I really fucked up this time. I really did. *(Sitting on a swivel chair, Eddie reaches around the counter to soak a towel in the sink. Phil is filling the coffee pot.)*

Eddie: You had a fight. So what? Give her a little time and call her up, you know that. Don't be so goddamn negative.

Phil: This was a big one.

Eddie: Bigger than the last one?

Phil: Yeah.

Eddie: So what'd you do, shoot her? *(He covers his face with the wet towel. Silence, as Phil is putting the coffee into the filter for the coffee machine. Eddie peeks out from behind the towel.)* You didn't shoot her, Phil. You got a gun?

Phil: On me?

Eddie: You didn't shoot her, Phil.

Phil: No.

Eddie *(He puts the towel back over his face, pressing it against his eyes)*: So, she'll take you back. She always takes you back.

Phil: Not this time.

Eddie *(Bursting out from behind the towel, he begins rummaging around the counter for aspirin, which he finds)*: What happened?

Phil: I went too far. She ain't going to take me back.

Eddie: You want me to call her?

Phil: She'll give you the fucking business. She hates you.

Eddie: Whata you mean, she hates me?

Phil: She hates you.

Eddie: What are you talking about, she hates me? Susie don't hate me. She likes me.

Phil: She hates you; she told me.

Eddie: She hates me? How can she hate me?

Phil: She hates you. She tol' me. In the middle of the fight.

Eddie *(His head killing him, takes some aspirin)*: What are you talking about: you two are in the middle of this bloodbath—the goddamn climactic go-round of your seven-year career in, you know what I mean, marital carnage and somewhere in the peak of this motherfucker she takes time out to tell you she hates good ol' Eddie. Am I supposed to believe that?

Phil: I was surprised too. I thought she liked you.

Eddie: You're serious.

Phil: Yeah.

Eddie: So fuck her. What a whore. She hates me. Are you serious? This is unacceptable goddamn behavior.

Phil: She's unbelievable.

Eddie *(Rising, he is kicking at his slacks, stepping on them to get them off, and starting toward the stairs and the bathroom)*: This is unbelievable. I mean, what is she, a goddamn schizophrenic, here? Is this a goddamn psychotic we've been dealing with here? I mean, isn't she always friendly with me? You have seen this, right? I mean, I'm not a goddamn imbecile to have thought she liked me. She acted like she liked me.

Phil *(Following after Eddie)*: I thought she liked me.

Eddie *(As they climb the stairs together)*: I thought she liked you, too. I mean, she don't like anybody, is that the situation, the pathetic bitch?

Phil: I knew she hated Artie.

Eddie: I knew she hated Artie, too. *(He goes into the bathroom.)* But Artie's an obnoxious, anal obsessive pain in the ass who could make his best friend hire crazed, unhappy people with criminal tendencies to cut off his legs, which we have both personally threatened to do. So she hates a guy who, though we both love him, we both personally know it is somewhat in spite of him that we love him. So that proves nothing. *(There is the sound of the toilet flushing and then Eddie, carrying a pair of jogging* *shorts, steps back into the hallway.)* I mean, what the hell does she think gives her justification to hate me?

Phil: She didn't say.

Eddie: She didn't say?

Phil: No. *(He goes into the bathroom.)*

Eddie *(Pulling on the jogging shorts)*: She gave no rhyme nor reason? She just—you gotta help me picture this—she what? In the middle of some goddamn retort, or was it out of the blue?

Phil: Whata you mean?

Eddie: I mean, did she have a point of reference, some sort of reference from within your blowup out of which she made some goddamn association which was for her justification that she come veering off to dump all this unbelievable vituperative horseshit over me—whatever it was. I wanna get it straight. *(Toilet is flushed, and Phil comes out of the bathroom.)*

Phil: You got some weed? I need some weed. *(Followed by Phil, Eddie heads down the stairs to the kitchen counter where he pulls from a shelf his drug box and, opening it, takes out a rolled joint.)*

Eddie: I got great weed. You wanna toke up?

Phil: I need somethin'.

Eddie *(Handing a joint to Phil)*: You just help me out, all right; I got to get this straight.

Phil: I'm tryin', Eddie. You know that.

Eddie *(As Phil inhales, trying to remember, Eddie sits Phil down on the swivel chair outside the counter)*: So what'd she say about me? You know, think back. So the two of you are hurling insults and she's a bitch, blah, blah, blah, you're a bastard, rapateta. *(Moving to serve coffee to Phil.)* So in the midst of this TUMULT where do I come in?

Phil *(Remembering suddenly)*: You're just like me, she says.

Eddie: What? *(At the coffee, he freezes mid-gesture.)* We're alike? She said that?

Phil: Yeah—we were both whatever it was she was calling me at the time.

Eddie: I mean, that's sad. She's sad. They're all sad. They're all fucking crazy. What is she thinking about?

Phil: I don't know.

Eddie: What do you think she's thinking about?

Phil: We're friends. You know. So she thinks we got somethin' in common. It's logical.

Eddie: But we're friends on the basis of what, Phil? On the basis of opposites, right? We're totally dissimilar is the basis of our friendship, right?

Phil: Of course.

Eddie: I mean, I been her friend longer than I been yours. What does she think, that I've been—what? More sympathetic to you than her in these goddamn disputes you two have? If that's what she thought she should have had the guts to tell me, confront me!

Phil: I don't think that's what she thought.

Eddie: SO WHAT WAS IT?

Phil: I don't know. I don't think she thinks.

Eddie (*Settling onto the swivel chair opposite Phil*): None of them think. I don't know what they do.

Phil: They don't think.

Eddie: They calculate. They manipulate. So what's she up to? They express their feelings. I mean, my feelings are hurt, too.

Phil (*Growing frenzied*): Mine, too.

Eddie: They're all nuts.

Phil (*And more frenzied*): I pity them, I fuckin' pity them. She makes me crazy. I ain't gonna see her any more.

Eddie: This is terrible on a certain level. I mean, I liked you two together.

Phil (*Agitated, starting to pace away from Eddie*): I know. Me, too. A lot of people did. I'm very upset. Let me have some more weed. (*Reaching back he grabs the joint from Eddie, then immediately paces on, roaming the living room.*) It was terrible. It was somethin'. Blah-blah-blah!

Eddie: Rapateta. Hey, absolutely.

Phil: Blah-blah-blah! You know, I come home in the middle 'a the night—she was out initially with her girlfriends, so naturally I was alone and went out too. So I come home, I'm ripped, I was on a tear, but I'm harmless, except I'm on a talking jag, you know, who cares? She could have some sympathy for the fact that I'm ripped, she could take that into consideration, let me run my mouth a little, I'll fall asleep, where's the problem? That's what you would do for me, right?

Eddie: Yeah.

Phil (*Rushing to Eddie to hand him the joint*): She can't do that.

Eddie: What's she do? What the hell's the matter with her, she can't do that?

Phil: I'm on a tear, see, I got a theory how to take Las Vegas and turn it upside down like it's a little rich kid and shake all the money out of its pockets, right?

Eddie: Yeah. So what was it?

Phil: It was bullshit, Eddie. (*Sitting back down opposite Eddie.*) I was demented and totally ranting, so to that extent she was right to pay me no attention, seriously, but she should of faked it. But she not only sleeps, she snores. So I gotta wake her up, because, you know, the most important thing to me is that, in addition to this Las Vegas scam, I have this theory on the Far East, you know; it's a kind of vision of Global Politics, how to effect a real actual balance of power. She keeps interrupting me. You know, I'm losing my train of thought everytime she interrupts me. It's a complex fucking idea, so I'm asking her to just have some consideration until I get the whole thing expressed, then she wants to have a counterattack, I couldn't be more ready.

Eddie: She won't do that?

Phil: No.

Eddie: That's totally uncalled for, Phil. All you're asking for is civilization, right? You talk and she talks. That's civilization, right? You take turns!

Phil: I don't think I'm asking for anything unusual, but I don't get it.

Eddie: Perverse.

Phil: Perverse is what she wrote the book on it. I am finally going totally crazy. *(Jumping back up on his feet.)* I've totally lost track of my ideas. I'm like lookin' into this hole in which was my ideas. I arrive thinkin' I can take Vegas and save the world. Forty-five seconds with her and I don't know what I'm talking about. So I tell her—"LISTEN! —lemme think a second, I gotta pick up the threads." She says some totally irrelevant but degrading shit about my idea and starts some nitpicking with which she obviously intends to undermine my whole fucking Far Eastern theory on the balance of powers, and I'm sayin', "Wait a minute," but she won't. So WHACK! I whack her one in the face. Down she goes.

Eddie: You whacked her.

Phil: I whacked her good. You see my hand. *(Moving to Eddie, Phil holds out his hand.)*

Eddie *(Rising to look at Phil's hand)*: You did that to your hand?

Phil: Her fuckin' tooth, see.

Eddie *(Teasing Phil a little)*: You were having this political discussion with which she disagreed, so you whacked her out, is that right?

Phil: It wasn't the politics. I didn't say it was the politics.

Eddie: What was it? You were ripped?

Phil: Yeah. But it wasn't that. I don't know what it was. *(Phil sits down on the couch, starts to play with a toy, a magic cube sitting on the table.)*

Eddie: What was it? *(Moving to sit beside Phil.)*

Phil: I don't know. I had this idea and then it was gone.

Eddie *(Eager)*: Yeah.

Phil: It was just this disgusting cloud like fucking with me and I went crazy.

Eddie *(Delighted)*: Right. Whata you mean?

Phil: You know this fog, and I was in it and it was talking to me with her face on it. Right in front of me was like this cloud with her face on it, but it wasn't just her, but this cloud saying all these mean things about my ideas and everything about me, so I was like shit and this cloud knew it. There was no way out. I couldn't get my thoughts together. They were all over the place. And once they were all over the place they weren't anything any more. That was when it happened.

Eddie: You whacked her.

Phil: Yeah.

Eddie: Was she all right?

Phil: She was scared, and I was scared. I don't know if I was yelling I would kill her or she was yelling she was going to kill me.

Eddie: Somebody was threatening somebody, though.

Phil: Definitely.

Eddie *(Rising, he paces in a meditative, investigative manner across the room for more coffee)*: So try and remember how was it before you whacked her or after you whacked her that she made her reference to me?

Phil: You mean that she hated you?

Eddie: Yeah.

Phil: Before. It was in the vicinity of Vegas, I think, but it gets blurry.

Eddie: So what musta happened is she decided I had some connection to your Vegas scam and this was for her justification to dump all this back-stabbing hostility all over me.

Phil: She didn't say that. She just says we're both assholes.

Eddie: But it would be logical that if this petty, cheap-shot animosity was in the vicinity of Vegas, it would have to do with Vegas. THAT WOULD ONLY BE LOGICAL.

Phil: EXCEPT SHE AIN'T LOGICAL.

Eddie: True.

Phil: SHE'S JUST A NASTY BITCH AND I MARRIED HER.

Eddie: You know what I think?

Phil: What?

Eddie: She hates men.

Phil (*Crossing toward Eddie, very interested*): Whata you mean?

Eddie: She hates you, she hates me. She hates men. I don't know what else to think. It's a goddamn syllogism. Susie hates Phil, Susie hates Eddie. She hates men.

Phil: And Artie, too.

Eddie: Artie, Eddie, Phil are men, she hates men. The fucker's irrefutable, except that's not how it works, GODDAMNIT.

Phil: What?

Eddie: You go from the general to the particular. I'm talking about a syllogism, here.

Phil: Yeah.

Eddie (*Irritated, storming off, he slumps into the big armchair, the better to think*): Damnit! What the hell goes the other way?

Phil: Which way?

Eddie: Something goes the other goddamn way!

Phil: What?

Eddie: You start from the particular in something. Susie hates Eddie, Susie hates Phil. Phil and Eddie are men, therefore, blah, blah, blah. . . . Oh, my god, do you know what it is?

Phil: What?

Eddie: Science! What goes the other way is science, in which you see all the shit like data and go from it to the law. This is even better. We have just verified, and I mean scientifically, the bitch has been proven to basically hate all men. She doesn't need a reason to hate me in particular—she already hates me in the fucking abstract.

Phil: You gonna call her?

Eddie: You want me to?

Phil: You said you were gonna!

Eddie: That was before I understood the situation. Now that I understand the situation, the hell with her. The bitch wants to go around hating me in the fucking abstract! Are you nuts? Call her? I wouldn't piss on her if the flames were about to engulf her goddamn, you know, central nervous system! *(As Mickey staggers out of his bedroom onto the balcony, Phil grabs up a bottle of bourbon from the counter.)*

Phil: I am going to hole up here and ossify myself.

Eddie: I MEAN, WHERE THE HELL DOES SHE GET OFF? *(It is important to note that there is an element of play in this whole scene between Phil and Eddie: on some level it is a game, a riff and that Eddie tends to adopt Phil's mannerisms when alone with him.)*

Mickey: Didn't I beg you to let me have some goddamn quiet this morning? Eddie, I begged you!

Eddie *(Runs to the base of the stairs, yelling up)*: Phil has left Susie again, only this time it's final!

Mickey: So what are YOU screaming about?

Phil *(Following after Eddie)*: The deceitful bitch has been bad-mouthing Eddie. That's been part of the problem from the beginning.

Eddie: Her attitude has been deceitful and degrading!

Mickey: So when did this happen?

Phil: It's been goin' on.

Mickey: It'll blow over. *(Mickey goes reeling into the bathroom.)*

Eddie: No!

Phil: I don't think so.

Eddie *(Having a fit at the base of the stairs, yet there is a note of sheer delight in it)*: I mean, she thinks she can do this shit and get away with it? He goes back, he's nuts. He deserves her. You go back this time, Phil, I'm never gonna speak to you again.

Phil: I know that. I agree with you.

Mickey *(Coming out of the bathroom)*: He's not serious, Phil.

Eddie: Whata you know about it?

Mickey: You're serious, if Phil goes back to his wife, you don't ever want to speak to him again? *(Descending the stairs, Mickey is all but attacked by Eddie.)*

Eddie: I'm serious. *(As Mickey moves to the kitchen, Eddie and Phil follow him, both yelling at Mickey and one another, an element of fun between them that they are tormenting Mickey with their noise and craziness when he has just awoken.)*

Mickey: That's not serious.

Eddie: Says you! I know when I'm serious and I'm serious, and Phil knows it even if you don't.

Phil: I hate her anyway!

Eddie: See! And you'd know it, too, if you were my goddamn friend like you think you are.

Phil: I'm done with her!

Eddie *(Grabbing his box of cocaine and other drugs from its shelf under the breakfast nook counter)*: See!

Mickey: You guys are in a fucking frenzy here. Have some breakfast, why don't you? Eat an orange, why don't you? Calm you down. We need some fruit in this house. Where's the fruit? *(As Mickey looks in the refrigerator, Eddie has handed a vial of coke to Phil and has spread a line for himself on the countertop. Phil hovers beside Eddie.)* Where's the food? We need some food in this house. Eddie, where's all the food? *(Seeing Eddie preparing to snort some cocaine.)* What are you doing?

Eddie: What's it look like I'm doin'?

Mickey: It looks like—What does it look like? It looks like you are doin' a line of coke on the kitchen counter here at eight forty-five in the morning.

Eddie: Very good. *(Eddie and Phil snort coke and exchange glances and pokes throughout this, clearly a conspiracy against Mickey; almost like two bad little boys with a baby-sitter they don't much respect.)*

Mickey: What are you becoming, a coke fiend, Eddie?

Eddie: How'm I gonna wake up? I gotta wake up!

Mickey: Some people have coffee.

Eddie: The caffeine is fucking poison, don't you know that?

Mickey: Right. So what is this, Bolivian health food? Some people risk it with coffee to wake up in the morning, rather than this shit which can make you totally chemically insane. Don't you watch the six o'clock news?

Eddie: I watch all the news.

Mickey *(Looking under the counter, he finds a package of English muffins containing two muffins which he waves with a flourish)*: Bread. I found some fucking bread. All right, we can have some muffins for breakfast. We can have some mouldy muffins along with our Bolivian Blow for breakfast. How long have I slept? Last time I saw you, you were a relatively standard every-day alcoholic Yahoo, Eddie. Now the bread's mouldy and you're sniffin' around the goddamn breakfast nook like a wart hog.

Eddie: I had a rough night. Whata you want from me?

Mickey: You should go to bed. *(Mickey is cutting a muffin, putting butter and jelly on it.)*

Eddie: How'm I going to get to bed?

Mickey: I don't know. Most people manage it. I don't know. Is this an outrageous suggestion, that he should get to bed? He's

down here half the night, Phil, crashing around and talking to
the TV like a goddamn maniac. Want half a dead English muffin, Phil? *(Offering jellied muffins on a plate to Phil, who looks at
Eddie, and Mickey shifts the plate toward Eddie.)* Eddie?

Eddie *(Clearly snubbing Mickey, Eddie turns to Phil, who is spooning
coke from the vial)*: I gotta wake up. *(As Phil puts the coke to one of
Eddie's nostrils.)* I got a lot of work today. *(Phil puts coke to Eddie's
other nostril and Eddie snorts, then grabs Phil's face between his
hands.)* The shit that went down here last night was conspira-
torial. It was unbelievable. *(Eddie walks toward the front door, Phil
following along.)* I mean, first of all the eleven o'clock news has
just devastated me with this shitload of horror in which it
sounds like not only are we headed for nuclear devastation if
not by the Russians then by some goddamn primitive bunch of
middle-eastern motherfuckers—*(Opening the front door, he
reaches out and picks up several newspapers, glancing at them as he
talks to Phil. Mickey, abandoned in the kitchen nook, eats the muffins.)*—and I don't mean that racially but just culturally, because they are so far back in the forest in some part of their
goddamn mental sophistication, they are likely to drop the
bomb just to see the light and hear the big noise. I mean, I am
talking not innate ability, but sophistication here. They have
got to get off the camels and wake up! *(Handing the newspapers
to Phil, Eddie starts up the stairs.)* So on top of this, there's this
accidental electrical fire in which an entire family is inciner-
ated, the father trying to save everybody by hurling them out
the window, but he's on the sixth floor, so he's, you know—
they're like eggs on the sidewalk. So much for heroics. *(Having
paused partway up the stairs, he now pivots to hasten up the remain-
der.)* So then my wife calls! You wanna have some absurdity?

Phil: I thought you was divorced.

Eddie: I am.

Phil: You said, "wife."

Eddie *(Pausing on the balcony to look down)*: Why would I do that?
I hate my ex-wife. I might have said "mother" instead of "ex-
wife," but not "wife."

Phil: Why would you do THAT?

Eddie (*Playfully exasperated*): Because I could have made a Freudian slip!

Phil: You don't believe in that shit, do you?

Eddie: Whata you know about it?

Phil: Somethin'. I know somethin'. I was in prison.

Eddie (*Going into his room*): Mickey, what'd I say?

Mickey: I wasn't listening.

Phil (*With all the newspapers, he sits on the arm of the couch and yells up at Eddie's door*): I mean, how would that shit work? You'd have WHAT?—all that stuff from your neighborhood like chasing you?

Mickey: You mean like from your background.

Phil: You believe in that Freudian shit, Mickey?

Mickey: What Freudian shit?

Phil: You know. All those books!

Mickey: No.

Phil: Me neither. (*Crossing to join Mickey.*) I mean, how would that work? What? Ghosts?

Mickey: It wouldn't.

Phil: So assholes pay all this money, right. (*As Eddie, having come out of his room, buttoning a clean shirt but still wearing the jogging shorts, is descending the stairs.*) It's unbelievable; and it don't work.

Mickey: Eddie's done it.

Phil: You done it, Eddie?

Eddie (*Taking a newspaper from Phil*): What?

Phil: What we're talkin' about here. You were just talkin' about it, too!

Mickey: Freud.

Eddie *(As he settles in the armchair to read)*: Right. One of the real prestige guys of blow. A pioneer. *(And opening the paper, he closes the conversation.)*

Mickey: So, Phil, you left your wife. I liked your wife.

Phil: You can have her. *(Rising, he moves off to the couch carrying what's left of the newspapers.)*

Mickey: Don't kid yourself. You find anybody whatsoever with her when you go back, let alone me, of whom your affection is borderline to say the least, you'll kill them.

Phil: I ain't going back.

Mickey: So your personal life's a shambles, how's your career?

Phil: I'm up for some very interesting parts at the moment, and on several of them—my agent says on this new cop show for NBC, my agent says I'm a lock, that's how close I am. I been back six times; the director and I have hit it off. It's very exciting.

Mickey: Who's the director?

Phil: He's this terrific Thomas Leighton.

Eddie *(Quite exasperated)*: This is the Thomas Leighton thing? *(It is clearly a topic he put time and energy in trying to make clear for Phil.)* He's a scumbag, I tol' you, Phil. He's a scumbag faggot who likes to jerk tough guys like you around. He'll bring you back a hundred times, you'll get nothing.

Phil *(A little distressed that Eddie is saying these things in front of Mickey)*: My agent says he likes me, and it's between me and this other guy who is taller, and that the only problem is when they cast the lead, if he's a different physical type than me, then I'll have a very good shot.

Eddie: The leads are always a different physical type than you, Phil. This is America. This is TV.

Phil *(Leaping to his feet, he bolts for the door)*: What are you tryin' to discourage me for?

Eddie *(Rushing to stop Phil from leaving)*: I'm not trying to discourage you.

Mickey (*Easing toward the stairs*): This is Eddie's particular talent—to effortlessly discourage people.

Eddie (*His hand on Phil, he almost follows Mickey up the stairs so urgent is his point*): If Phil wants to obliquely pick my brain about our area of expertise here, Mickey, am I supposed to pretend that you and I are not casting directors or I haven't noticed the whys and wherefores of how the thing happens in this town? I mean, right, Phil?

Phil (*A little like a kid on a street corner, he hangs around one of the balcony support beams*): I mean, Eddie, I trust that you are not deliberately trying to discourage me, but in all honesty, I gotta tell you, I'm feelin' very discouraged.

Eddie (*Genuinely wanting to impart sincere and friendly wisdom to Phil*): No, no. Look, you have to exploit your marketable human qualities, that's all. You have certain qualities and you have to exploit them. I mean, basically we all know the M.O. out here is they take an interesting story, right? They distort it, right? Cut whatever little truth there might be in it out on the basis of it's unappealing, but leave the surface so it looks familiar—cars, hats, trucks, trees. So, they got their scam, but to push it they have to flesh it out, so this is where you come in, because then they need a lot of authentic sounding and looking people—high-quality people such as yourself, who need a buck. So like every other whore in this town, myself included, you have to learn to lend your little dab of whatever truth you can scrounge up in yourself to this total, this systematic sham—so that the fucking viewer will be exonerated from ever having to confront directly the fact that he is spending his life face to face with total shit. So that's all I'm sayin'. "Check with me," is all I'm sayin'. Forget about this Leighton thing. (*Together, they have ended up back by the couch and TV.*)

Phil: Forget about it? I got nothin' else to do. What about the things you're currently working on? Anything for me?

Mickey (*Descending the steps, dressed for work, and carrying a handful of résumés and photographs*): Nothing.

Phil: Who asked you? (*Mickey settles down on the window seat to sort the résumés.*)

Eddie: There's a thing down the road a month or so, it might be a good thing for you. *(He crosses to the breakfast nook counter where scripts are piled on shelves.)*

Phil: What is it?

Eddie: It's a special or a pilot, they haven't decided. *(Picking a joint from an ashtray on the counter, he prepares to light up.)*

Phil: But there might be somethin' in it for me. You got a script? *(He strides over and takes the script that Eddie is pulling from the pile.)*

Eddie: This is shit, though. I don't wanna hear about the quality, because this is total shit. *(He inhales the joint.)*

Mickey: Don't get fucked up, Eddie. We got that meeting with the guy.

Eddie: So maybe you could handle things alone this morning? Whataya think?

Mickey: I think they're expecting both of us, that's what I think.

Phil *(Leaning against the wall, he has been leafing through the script)*: This is shit, huh?

Eddie: Total.

Phil: But there might be somethin' in it for me?

Eddie: Yeah. *(Phil, grabbing his coat, starts off. Eddie jumps after him, fearful Phil's feelings have been hurt again.)* Where you goin'?

Phil *(Indicating the stairs)*: I'm going to read it. And also, I'm beat. I'm really beat. It's been one exhausting thing I went through. I'm gonna pass out in your room, Eddie, okay?

Eddie *(As Phil is going up the stairs)*: We'll do something later. *(Eddie takes a huge toke on the joint.)*

Mickey: Do you realize, Eddie, that you are now toking up at eight fifty-eight in the morning on top of the shit you already put up your nose? You're going to show up at work looking like you got a radish for a nose. You're going to show up talking like a fish.

Eddie: Don't worry about it, okay?

Mickey: Is that supposed to fuck me up? *(Mickey moves from the window seat to the couch where he sits.)*

Eddie: You don't have to worry about me, Mickey.

Mickey: What kind of tone is that?

Eddie: What do you mean, what kind of tone is that? That's my tone.

Mickey: So what does it mean?

Eddie: My tone? What does my tone mean? I don't have to interpret my fucking tone to you, Mickey. I don't know what it means. What do you think it means?

Mickey: Just don't get clandestine on me, Eddie; that's all I'm saying.

Eddie: But there are not a lot of dynamite ladies around anywhere you look, Mickey, as we both know, and I am the one who met Darlene first. I am the one who brought her by, and it was obvious right from the get-go that Darlene was a dynamite lady, this was a very special lady.

Mickey: We hit it off, Eddie, you know. I asked you.

Eddie *(All ease and smiles, he seems to be only after clarity)*: Absolutely. Look, I'm not claiming any reprehensible behavior on anybody's part, but don't ask me not to have my feelings hurt, okay. I'm not saying anything went on behind my back or I was deceived or anything. Nevertheless, the situation has had an effect on me. I mean, we are all sophisticated people, and Darlene and I most certainly had no exclusive commitment of any kind whatsoever to each other, blah-blah-blah.

Mickey *(Moving to the kitchen to get some coffee, he is relieved at their agreement)*: That's exactly what I'm saying. Rapateta.

Eddie: There's no confusion here, Mickey, but have a little empathy for crissake. *(Mickey nods, for "empathy" is certainly something he can afford to give.)* I bring this very special lady to my house to meet my roommate, my best friend, and I haven't been interested in a woman for years, seriously, I have this horror show of a marriage in my background, and everybody knows it, so blah-blah-blah, they have THIS ATTRACTION to each other. *(Seeing now that Eddie is after more than "empathy," Mickey pretends exasperation and bows his head to the counter in mock self-abasement.)* My roommate and my new girl—I'm just trying to tell the story here, Mickey; nobody's to blame. *(Patting Mickey on the back.)* Certainly not you. I mean, you came to me, you had experienced these vibes between yourself and Darlene— isn't that what you said?—I mean, you correct me if I'm wrong—but would I mind, you wondered, if you and Darlene had dinner in order to, you know, determine the nature of these vibes, or would that bother me? That's a fair—I mean, reasonable representation of what you asked.

Mickey *(Moving out with his coffee toward the armchair, he addresses invisible masses—his voice, of course, slightly self-mocking, not totally, by any means, serious)*: I just—I mean, from my point of view, the point is—the main point is, I asked.

Eddie: I know this.

Mickey: That—in my opinion—is the paramount issue, the crucial issue. And I don't want it forgotten.

Eddie *(Though charming, he is not without an ominous note in his tone and smile)*: Nothing from yesterday is forgotten, Mickey. You don't have to worry about that.

Mickey: Why do we have to go through this? I just wanna have some breakfast. I mean, couldn't you have said, "no"? Couldn't you have categorically, definitively said "no" when I asked? But you said—"Everybody's free, Mickey." That's what you said.

Eddie: Everybody is free.

Mickey: So what's this then?

Eddie: This? You mean this? This conversation?

Mickey: Yeah.

Eddie: This is JUST ME trying to maintain a, you know, viable relationship with reality. I'm just trying to make certain I haven't drifted off into some, you know, solitary paranoid fantasy system of my own, totally unfounded and idiosyncratic invention. I'm just trying to stay in reality, Mickey, that's all. Don't you want me to be in reality? I personally want us both to be in reality.

Mickey: Absolutely. That's what I want. *(And Mickey almost rushes to the chair opposite Eddie at the counter, as if with this move he will end the conversation on this note.)* I mean, I want us both to be in reality. Absolutely.

Eddie *(Very reassuring)*: So that's what's going on here, you know, blah-blah-blah. Don't take it personally.

Mickey *(Very affirmative)*: Blah-blah-blah!

Eddie: So I was just wondering. You came in this morning at something like six-oh-two, so your dinner must have been quite successful. These vibes must have been serious. I mean, sustaining, right?

Mickey: Right. Yeah. You know.

Eddie: Or does it mean—and I'm just trying to get the facts straight here, Mickey—does it mean you fucked her?

Mickey: Darlene?

Eddie: Right.

Mickey: Darlene? Did I fuck Darlene? Last night? Eddie, hey, I asked you. I thought we were clear on this thing.

Eddie: We're almost clear.

Mickey *(With a take-charge manner, as if he has at last figured out what it is that Eddie wants)*: What I mean, Eddie is, THINGS HAPPEN, but if this bothers you, I mean, if this bothers you, I don't have to see her again. This is not worth our friendship, Eddie; you know that.

Eddie *(Recoiling in a mockery of shock, yet not without a real threat)*: Wait a minute. You're not saying that you took my new girl, my very special dynamite girl out and fucked her on a whim, I mean, a fling and it meant nothing!? You're not saying that?

Mickey: No, no, no.

Eddie: I mean, these vibes were serious, right? These vibes were the beginnings of something very serious, right? They were the first, faint, you know, things of a serious relationship, right?

Mickey: Hey, whatever.

Eddie (*Munching the remnants of one of the muffins, he is quite happy*): I mean, I don't want to interfere with any possibilities for happiness in your life, Mickey.

Mickey: Believe me, this is not a possibility for happiness in my life.

Eddie: Well, it was in mine. It was such a possibility in mine.

Mickey: I think you just have it maybe all out of proportion here, Eddie.

Eddie: Yeah? So do me a breakdown.

Mickey: I just think maybe she's not as dynamite as you might think. (*Mickey's remark nearly catapults Eddie across the room.*)

Eddie: Fuck you!

Mickey: You always go a little crazy about women, Eddie.

Eddie: You wanna let it alone, Mickey.

Mickey: It's not a totally, you know, eccentric thing to happen to a guy, so don't get fucking defensive.

Eddie: I mean, there's nothing here that necessitates any sort of underground smear campaign against Darlene.

Mickey: No, no, no. I just want you to think about the possibility that things have gotten a little distorted, that's all.

Eddie: No.

Mickey: You won't think about it?

Eddie: I mean, bad-mouthing her just to get yourself off the hook—don't think you can do that.

Mickey: Never.

Eddie: It's not that I DON'T understand—it's that I DO understand. It's just that I'm not so fucking sophisticated as to be totally beyond this entire thing, you see what I'm saying, Mickey. Blah-blah-blah—my heart is broken—blah-blah-blah. *(He flops down on the couch, as if he might go back to sleep.)*

Mickey: Blah—blah—blah. Absolutely. So you want me to toast you what's left of the muffin? We can put some raisins on it—be a sort of Danish. Somebody's got to go shopping.

Eddie: You think we couldn't handle a dog around here?

Mickey: I wouldn't want to be a fucking dog around here. Dogs need stability.

Eddie: I like dogs.

Mickey *(As he goes into the kitchen to start cleaning up the mess there)*: You could borrow Artie's dog.

Eddie: I hate Artie's dog. It looks like a rat; it doesn't look like a dog. I like big dogs.

Mickey: So did you get any sleep at all?

Eddie: Fucking Agnes had to call. Why does she have to call?

Mickey: Why do you talk to her is the real question?

Eddie: I have to talk to her. We have a kid.

Mickey: That's a thought to turn the mind to pure jello—you or any man daring to get that close to Agnes. Are you sure you did it?

Eddie: Only with a borrowed cock.

Mickey: I mean, you might as well put your balls in her teeth as pick up the phone.

Eddie: Because she thinks she's smarter than me; she thinks I'm afraid of her and that I agree with her assessment of what went wrong between us.

Mickey *(Quite superior)*: But every time you talk to her, you end up in this total, this absolute nonproductive shit-fit over what she said, or meant, or might have been implying, and in the process deliver her conclusive proof of what for her is already irrefutable—namely that you're a mess. *(As Artie and Donna come in the front door.)* And then you go crazy for days!

Eddie: What do you want me to do, abandon my kid in her hands and with no other hope? Forget about it! *(He is turning over as if to hide his head or go to sleep, so he doesn't see Artie or Donna.)*

Artie is about ten years older than Eddie and Mickey. He is slick in appearance, dressed very California; a mix of toughness and arrogance, a cunning desperation; he carries a shoulder satchel or briefcase. With him is Donna; blonde, about fifteen. Carrying a Walkman Tape Player, she has earphones on. Under her arm she has a record album which she will carry everywhere. She wears tattered shorts, a T-shirt, a buckskin jacket, and beat-up cowboy boots. Seeing Artie, Mickey addresses him as if he's been standing there for years.

Mickey: Artie, so what's the haps, here?

Artie: You guys in the middle of something, or what?

Mickey: You didn't tell us you got married.

Artie: Her? I found her on the elevator.

Donna: Where's the bathroom?

Eddie: What kind of accent is that? What kind of accent you got?

Donna: I'm from the Midwest, so that's it.

Artie *(To Mickey)*: You want her?

Mickey: Whata you mean?

Artie: It's too crowded, see?

Donna: Artie, they got a bathroom?

Artie: Sure they got a bathroom.

Eddie *(From the couch)*: What's she want with our bathroom, Artie? Is this a goddamn coke fiend you brought with you here?

Donna: I gotta go.

Eddie: Where?

Donna: I gotta go to the bathroom.

Artie: This is Eddie.

Donna: Hi, you got a bathroom?

Eddie: It's upstairs.

Donna: Great.

Mickey *(As Donna hurries up the stairs)*: I'm Mickey. It's the first door.

Donna: Great, Mickey. I'm Donna. *(She goes into the bathroom, shutting the door.)*

Mickey: Cute, Artie, very cute.

Artie *(To Mickey)*: You want her?

Eddie: You keep sayin' that, Artie.

Artie *(As if irritated at her)*: She was on the goddamn elevator. In the hotel. I'm going out for coffee in the morning, I take the elevator, there she is.

Mickey *(Moving to get Artie some coffee)*: You want coffee. We got coffee, muffins, coke and raisins.

Artie *(Glancing at his watch, he settles into the swivel chair in front of the counter)*: It's too early for breakfast, but I'll have some coffee. This was yesterday. So I come back from coffee, she's in the elevator. It's an hour. So that's a coincidence. Then I'm going out for dinner. Right? This is seven—eight hours later. She's in the elevator.

Mickey: She's livin' in the elevator.

Artie: Yeah, so after dinner, there she is. So I ask her: Is she livin' in the elevator? She says her boyfriend tried to kill her, so she's stayin' off the street.

Mickey *(Handing Artie the coffee, Mickey stands behind the counter, leaning on it toward Artie)*: Why'd he want to kill her?

Artie: She says he was moody. So, I took her in. But I figured, I don't need her, you know, like you guys need her. You guys are a bunch of desperate guys. You're very desperate guys, right? You can use her. So I figured on my way to the studio, I'd drop her by, you can keep her. Like a CARE package, you know. So you can't say I never gave you nothing.

Eddie *(From the couch)*: You're giving her to us?

Artie: Yeah.

Eddie: What are we going to do with her?

Artie: What do you want to do with her?

Eddie: Where's she from?

Mickey *(As if Eddie is an imbecile)*: What has that got to do with anything?

Eddie: I wanna know.

Mickey: Somewhere in the Middle West. I heard her.

Eddie: That could be anywhere.

Mickey: So what?

Eddie *(Crossing toward them to get coffee)*: I'm just trying to figure out what we're going to do with her. You wanna pay attention.

Artie *(Intervening on Mickey's behalf)*: What do you want, Eddie, an instruction manual? This is a perfectly viable piece of ass I have brought you, and you're acting totally like WHAT? What's going on here? Are we in sync or not?

Eddie: Like she'll be a pet, is that what you're saying, Artie?

Artie: Right.

Mickey *(Patting Artie, his arm ending up around Artie)*: Right.

Artie: You can keep her around. *(Artie and Mickey exchange a look with which to patronize Eddie.)*

Eddie: She'll be like this pet we can keep and fuck her if we want to?

Artie: Sure. Just to stay in practice. In case you run into a woman.

ACT ONE: SCENE ONE   39

Eddie: I guess he hasn't heard about Darlene. (*It is as if the name, "Darlene" is a punch from which Mickey reels.*) I guess you haven't heard about Darlene, Artie.

Artie: No. Is this important?

Eddie: Mickey has gotten involved with this truly dynamite bitch in a very serious relationship.

Mickey: Bullshit. (*Rising, Mickey escapes across the room to the window seat where he sits down, picking up a* Variety.)

Artie: Is this true, Mickey? Is this the same Darlene, Eddie? You had a Darlene.

Eddie (*Leaning across the counter to Artie*): What I'm inferring here, Artie, is that Mickey is unlikely to be interested in this bimbo you have brought by for fear of, you know, contaminating his feelings and catching some vile disease in addition.

Artie: So when did this happen, Mickey? You guys switched, or what? I miss everything. So you're in a serious relationship, Mickey. That's terrific.

Mickey: Except I ain't serious about anything, Artie, you know that. (*As Donna comes out of the bathroom and down the stairs, her shoes clumping loudly.*)

Eddie: You wanna live with us for a while, Donna?

Donna (*Pausing at the base of the stairs to look at Eddie*): Hmmmmmmmmmmmmmm?

Artie (*He crosses toward her, as Mickey comes up behind her*): Okay, I gotta go. All she has to do for me is go down to the hotel twice a day and walk my dog.

Mickey (*Arm around her*): Right. (*As he blows the word in her ear, Donna yelps and scurries several steps away.*)

Eddie: What if she runs away?

Artie: What do you want from me, Eddie, a guarantee? (*Draping an arm over her shoulder, Artie slides a hand under her shirt and fiddles with her breast.*) I can't guarantee her. She worked last time I used her. You want a guarantee, talk to the manufacturer. I'm not the manufacturer.

Eddie (*Settling down on the swivel chair and picking up the phone*): You're the retailer.

Artie: Frankly, from the look of you, what I am is a goddamn charity organization having some compassion on some pathetic fuck who is you, that's what I am. (*After all, Eddie sits there still in his jogging shorts, and his partially buttoned shirt.*) I'm having some generosity toward the heartbreaking desperation I encounter here every time I come by and have to look at you. You don't mind if I have a little mercy.

Eddie: So where you goin'? You goin' to the studio?

Artie: I said that.

Eddie: You didn't say what for.

Artie: You didn't ask what for. I got a meeting.

Eddie: You know what happens to you doesn't happen to normal people.

Artie: I did good deeds in an earlier lifetime. How do I know?

Eddie: Yeah, but being a highly developed bullshit artist does not normally translate into this kind of situation.

Artie: He's a blocked writer, and my stories about my life unblock him. You know, it was his idea, and secretly, I always dreamed of it.

Eddie: Dreamed of what?

Artie (*Advancing on Eddie, he leaves Donna*): Having an interesting life and a capacity to relate some of it does not constitute a criminal offense against you personally, Eddie.

Eddie: Hey, you're misinterpreting my whole slant here; forget about it.

Artie: I intend to forget about it.

Eddie: You're an ungrateful prick, Artie.

Artie *(In a state of total delight, he pats Eddie's cheek)*: I'm desperate. *(And he starts for the door.)*

Eddie: Just keep me informed. I want to be of help. You got a deal, right?

Artie *(The door open, his hand on the knob, he stops, and, looking back, he is very happy, very confident, almost grand: He will, it seems, soon own the entire town of Hollywood)*: Things look VERY good. They look VERY good. You know, who can tell in this town?

Eddie: Did they write the check? If they wrote the check, you got a deal.

Artie: So they didn't.

Eddie: Then you don't.

Artie: YET. They didn't YET.

Eddie: Then you don't YET. If they didn't YET, you don't YET.

Artie: But we're close. We're very close.

Eddie: The game in this town is not horseshoes, Artie.

Artie *(Rushing back to Eddie to make his point)*: How come you're being such a prick to me?

Eddie: Envy!

Artie: I didn't think you knew.

Eddie: Of course I know. What do you think, I don't know what I'm feeling?

Artie: It happens.

Eddie: Everything happens. *(Standing up, the phone still in his hand.)* But what I'm after here, I mean ultimately, is for your own good, for your clarity. You lose your clarity in this town next thing you know you're waking up in the middle of the night on the beach with dogs pissing on you, you think you're on vacation. You panic in this town, Artie, they can smell it in your sweat.

Artie: Who's gonna panic? I been learning these incredible, fantastic relaxation techniques.

Eddie (*Sitting back down, he begins dialing the phone*): Who's the producer you're most often in the room with?

Artie: Simon! He's got a distribution deal now with Universal.

Mickey: What relaxation techniques?

Artie: They are these ones that are fantastic, Mickey, in as much as you can do them under the table, you're in some goddamn meeting, you just tense your feet and—

Eddie: HERB Simon? HERB Simon? Is this who we're talking about? (*He slams down the phone.*)

Artie: What about him?

Eddie (*Standing, Eddie leans toward Artie like a fighter in his corner*): This is the guy you're dealing with? This guy's a known snake. I got the right guy, Artie. Herb Simon.

Artie: Yeh. Universal.

Eddie: THIS GUY'S AN ANACONDA. HE'S A KNOWN ANACONDA.

Artie: (*Shrugging, he's heard everything*): I heard that.

Eddie: I mean, you gotta make this guy pay you if you say "Hello" to him, right? You're not crossing the street free for this guy, are you?

Artie: We gotta do a treatment.

Eddie: No!

Artie: It's nothin'. He's a major guy. I don't want to piss him off.

Eddie: These fucking snakes are sharks out here, Artie, you know that.

Mickey: He's right, Artie.

Artie: We have hit it off, Mickey. He likes me.

Mickey: Good.

Eddie: If it's true, it's good.

Artie: Fuck you. The guy is at this juncture where he's sick of himself; he's looking for some kind of fucking turnaround into decency.

Eddie: You base this opinion on what, Artie, your desperate desire to succeed?

Artie: Something happened and I saw it, goddamnit.

Mickey: So what happened?

Artie: It was the other day after lunch.

Eddie: Who paid?

Artie (*Snapping at Eddie, snarling*): He did. He paid. (*And then back to Mickey, developing a manner of high confidence, his story that of an amazing and rare intimacy with a creature of almost royal importance.*) So we're crossing the street. You know, he gets this terrible pain in his stomach. I mean, his stomach made a noise and he doubles over like this. It's a noise like a gorilla could have made it. And he's over like this and he's paralyzed. We're all paralyzed in the middle of the street. So we get across the street. I'm asking him, is he okay. Maybe the food was bad. "No," he says. "Maybe," I says. "No. It's all the lies I tell," he says. He looks me in the eye and says, "It's this town and all the lies it makes me tell," See? He tol' me that.

Mickey: Herb Simon said that?

Artie: Yeah!

Eddie: So?

Artie (*Moving in righteous anger at Eddie*): So, he was straight with me, you cynical prick.

Eddie: So, what's the point? This fucking snake tells you he lies a lot, so you figure you can trust him? That's not clear, Artie. Wake up! This guy is legendary among snakes. He is permanently enshrined in the reptilian hall of Hollywood fucking fame, this guy. You don't wake up, they are going to eat you alive. As an appetizer! You won't even be the main course.

They're just going to whet their appetites on what is to you your entire motherfucking existence.

Artie *(Caught, his words are light little chunks of fury)*: You're making me nervous.

Eddie: I'm trying to make you nervous. Don't you know a ploy when you see one?

Artie: I considered whether it was a ploy, and I come down on the side of I would trust him a little.

Eddie: Why trust him at all?

Artie: I gotta work with him.

Eddie: You're not telling me you can't work with somebody you don't trust.

Artie: No.

Eddie: I'm not saying, "Don't work with him!" I'm saying, "Don't trust him!"

Artie: I'll talk to him! *(Looking at his watch, Artie panics and starts scurrying around, gathering his things.)*

Eddie: Get some money! Get some bucks!

Artie: For crissake, I'm gonna be late with this bullshit you put me through, Eddie. What do you do this to me for? He's gonna be pissed at me, goddamnit! *(He rushes out the door.)*

Donna: Bye, Artie.

Eddie: You think I was too hard on him?

Mickey: No.

Eddie: You gotta be hard on him, right?—he's a hard-head himself.

Mickey *(On the move toward Donna)*: So how is Goldilocks doing here? You had any breakfast? *(His fingers are in her hair.)*

Eddie *(Heading for the refrigerator)*: You want a beer?

Donna *(Rising, she moves toward the counter)*: Sure.

Eddie *(At the refrigerator)*: Where'd you say you were from?

Mickey *(Lighting a joint, he follows along after her)*: She said Midwest. I remember. Isn't that what you said?

Donna: Yeah.

Mickey: See.

Eddie *(Handing her a beer)*: So you came out here to get into the movies?

Donna: We were hitchhiking.

Mickey: Where to?

Donna: The Grand Canyon.

Eddie: It's not in L.A.

Donna: I just kept going.

Mickey: So you were in Artie's elevator? *(Having drawn the smoke in, he puts his mouth on Donna's and blows the smoke into her.)*

Donna: It wasn't his. Can I turn on the TV?

Eddie *(Imitating her accent)*: Sure. *(Donna goes scurrying to the TV, which she turns on and sits in front of.)* So if Artie hadn't invited you off the elevator, would you still be on it?!

Donna: I saw some interesting things I was on it!

Mickey *(Yelling over the loud volume of the TV)*: Like what?! *(He crosses to sit beside her on the couch.)*

Donna *(Yelling)*: Different people!

Eddie *(Yelling)*: This was interesting! *(Eddie crosses to stand leaning against the side of the armchair facing the couch.)*

Donna *(Yelling)*: You could hear their conversation! Some were about their rooms and the hotel carpeting, or the pictures in the hall! There was sometimes desperation you couldn't get a handle on it! They talked about their clothes! *(Mickey, reaching forward, turns off the volume of the TV.)*

Mickey: So you evidently would have starved to death mesmerized by the spellbinding panorama on this elevator, it wasn't for Artie.

Donna: I'da got off to eat. That's crazy. It was nice of Artie nevertheless to take a chance on me and everything. He's been just, you know, fantastic. (*Again Mickey puts his mouth to Donna's and blows the smoke into her, and then he pulls back.*) Except it is boring how he sits sometimes at the table, he's got these pencils, and he doesn't say anything to you. (*Moving to the floor, Mickey pulls her boot off, and her sock. She quickly grabs up her boot, clutching it.*) And he's got this paper, and I couldn't watch any TV except with the sound off because the noises would bother his train of thought. It was interesting for a while to watch TV in silence like old-time movies, except you didn't have a clue. (*When Mickey goes to work on her second boot, pulling it off, she grabs it from him, trying to interest him in her points about TV.*) You know, how they would put those words up every now and then in old-time movies so you could sort of hang on to the direction things were taking. And they acted like deaf people talking. Well, on TV there was none of these advantages, so I had to work up my own story a lot. (*As Mickey is reaching up to unbuckle the waist of her shorts, she leaps to her feet.*) Did he say what time I should walk his dog? (*Mickey grabs her arm to tug her back onto the couch while Eddie moves to take from her the record she carries.*)

Eddie: What's this?

Donna: It's just my favorite record for very particular reasons.

Eddie: Willie Nelson sings "Stardust," "Unchained Melody," "All of Me?"

Donna: Nobody ever agrees with me, people just scream at me.

Mickey: What?

Donna (*As she talks, Mickey, his arm around her, nuzzles her*): My friends, when I argue with them, they just scream at me, but it's these really terrific old songs sung by this new guy, right, Willie Nelson, only he's an old guy, and they're all like these big-city songs like Chicago or New York, right, Sinatra kind of songs, only Willie, who they are sung by, is this cowboy, so it's like this cowboy on the plains singing to his cows, and the mountains are there but it's still the deep, dark city streets, so it's like the mountains and the big sky are this nightclub in the night and this old cowboy, this old, old cowboy under a street light in the middle of the mountains is singing something old and modern, and it's everything, see. You wanna hear it?

Eddie: No.

Mickey: Sure. (*He kisses Donna, his hand moving to unbuckle her shorts as Eddie's bedroom door opens and Phil steps out, hair tousled, shirt off.*)

Phil: Anybody got any valium around here, Eddie?

Eddie: Look at this. Artie brought her by.

Phil: Where's Artie?

Mickey: He's gone.

Phil: Artie was here?

Eddie: Yeah.

Phil: Who's this?

Eddie: He brought her by for us. Like a CARE package. (*Reaching, Eddie takes Donna by the arm and lifts her from Mickey.*)

Phil: Yeah? Whata you mean?

Eddie: Not for Mickey, though.

Mickey (*Certain it's a joke*): Get off my back, you—

Eddie (*Arms around Donna*): This is for Phil and me because we don't have any serious relationships. This is a CARE package. Didn't you hear him? This is a CARE package for people without serious relationships.

Mickey: You prick.

Donna: What're you guys talking about?

Eddie: Fucking you.

Donna: Oh.

Eddie: Phil and me, but not Mickey because he has a serious relationship. He has to preserve it.

Donna: You gotta work at it, Mickey.

Phil: You're sayin' seriously this is includin' me?

Eddie: So we'll go upstairs, okay, Donna?

Donna (*A little stoned and scared*): Okay. (*She carries her boots and record as she and Eddie head for the stairs.*)

Phil: He can't, but I can?

Eddie: Yeah.

Mickey: You sonofabitch. (*Mickey is about to follow Eddie and Donna up the stairs.*)

Eddie (*Whirling at the base of the stairs to face Mickey*): Don't you even think about it. Right, Phil?

Mickey: I'll—(*Looking up, Mickey meets Phil's eyes.*) You jerk-off, Eddie! You jerk-off! I'll get her sometime you're not around.

Eddie (*Bounding up the stairs*): I can only do so much for you, Mickey. That'll be on your conscience.

Mickey: Give me a break.

Eddie (*Looking down on Mickey*): This is for your own good.

Phil (*Joining Eddie*): I got here just in time.

Eddie (*To Mickey*): You'll thank me later! (*And whirling, Eddie follows Donna into his room.*)

Mickey: You're nuts, Eddie; you're fucking nuts!

Phil: So this is the bachelor life!

Phil goes into the bedroom, slamming the door, and the MUSIC STARTS: Willie Nelson singing "All of Me" as Mickey stands, looking up for a beat, and the music plays.

BLACKOUT

The music continues.

SCENE TWO

TIME: Evening of the same day.

The music, Willie Nelson, singing "All of Me" continues. Darlene, beautiful and fashionable, is seated on one of the swivel chairs at the breakfast nook counter. Photography equipment is on the floor beside the chair. She is examining a contact sheet of photographs as the lights come up, and then the door opens and Eddie comes in dressed for work, carrying several scripts and a New York Times, *which he is reading as he walks, so he doesn't see Darlene. The music goes out.*

Darlene: Hi.

Eddie (*Though he is startled, we would never know it*): Hi, Darlene. Mickey around?

Darlene: I'm supposed to meet him. Is it okay?

Eddie: Sure. What?

Darlene: I was going to wait outside.

Eddie (*Heading for the refrigerator for a beer, he is all smiles*): What? Are you crazy? No, no, no. Sit down. How you doing? You look good.

Darlene: It's a facade.

Eddie: What isn't? That's what I meant, you know. I wasn't saying anything more. That's what I was saying. It's a terrifically successful facade. (*He sits in the swivel chair opposite her.*) So, how's life in the world of photojournalism, Darlene?

Darlene: Can I have a beer, too? I just feel . . . wow . . . you know?

Eddie: What?

Darlene: Weird, weird, weird.

Eddie: I mean, you're not giving this whole situation a second thought, are you?

Darlene: I certainly am. I . . .

Eddie: No, no, no.

Darlene: What situation? What do you mean? Do you—

Eddie: Us. Mickey, you, me. Us.

Darlene: Of course I am. That's what I thought you meant.

Eddie: Don't be crazy.

Darlene: Well, I have my mad side, you know. I have my feelings.

Eddie: I don't mean "mad" by "crazy." I mean, "mad" has a kind of grandeur about it. I mean more like "silly." Is that what I mean?

Darlene: Well, if you don't know, maybe you should stop talking till you figure it out and not go around just spewing out all this incomprehensible whatever it is you're saying and you know, hurting a person's feelings. That might have some value.

Eddie: I opted for spontaneity, you know.

Darlene: Well, sure. I'm just saying, "strike a balance."

Eddie: Is that what you were saying?

Darlene: Yes. That's right. What did you think I was saying?

Eddie: I mean, we've all had our feelings hurt. That's the one thing this situation has given us all in common, I would say. I would hope you're not trying to construct some unique, you know, strictly personal interpretation of things on that basis.

Darlene: What are you getting at?

Eddie: I'm not exactly certain.

Darlene: Well . . . are you exactly uncertain?

Eddie: Possibly.

Darlene: Where's Mickey?

Eddie: I haven't checked. Is he late?

Darlene: This is a perfect example of what could drive a person right off the wall about you. I mean, you are totally off the wall sometimes.

Eddie: In what way? Everybody has their flaws, Darlene.

Darlene *(Rising, she roots around in her camera case)*: This total way you exaggerate this enchantment you have with uncertainty—the way you just prolong it and expect us all to think we ought to try and live in it and it's meaningful. It's shit.

Eddie: This bothers you.

Darlene: It bothers everyone.

Eddie: No, it bothers you. And don't think this is a surprise. I am well aware of how what might to another person appear as honesty, but to you, it's—

Darlene: Some other person such as who?

Eddie: You want a list?

Darlene: I want an answer. And a beer.

Eddie: The beer is in the refrigerator. *(She storms past Eddie who lifts his knees up to his chest to make room for her as she rushes to the refrigerator.)* And the answer, if you want it from me, is coming along the lines I am speaking it, which is the only way it can come, since it's my answer, and if it is to come at all, it—

Darlene *(Charging past him with her beer)*: I don't have time. I mean, your thoughts are a goddamn caravan trekking the desert, and then they finally arrive and they are these senseless, you know, beasts, you know, of burden. Okay? So just forget about it.

Eddie: You asked me a question.

Darlene *(Pacing away from him)*: I also asked you to forget about it.

Eddie: But I don't want to forget about it.

Darlene: I made a mistake.

Eddie *(Rising)*: But you don't deny you asked it.

Darlene: Eddie, you look like a man with a hammer in his hand.

Eddie: So what? And I don't. Or are you a liar on top of everything else? You asked me a question!

Darlene: All right!

Eddie: Some sensitivity is the quality a person might have. Sure, I can come up with all the bullshit anytime—some clear-cut diagnosis totally without a solid, actual leg to stand on but presented with all the necessary postures and tones of voice full of conviction and all the necessary accessories and back-up systems of control and sincerity to lend total credibility to what is total bullshit; but I chose instead, and choose quite frequently, to admit it if I don't know what I'm talking about; or if I'm confused about what I'm feeling, I admit it. But this is too much of SOMETHING for you—I don't know what—so at least we found out in time. That's some good luck.

Darlene: Liar on top of WHAT ELSE?

Eddie: Whata you mean?

Darlene: You said, "liar on top of everything else."

Eddie: I did?

Darlene: Just a minute ago.

Eddie: What was I talking about?

Darlene: Me.

Eddie: I did? No. What'd I say? (*The front door opens, and Mickey, carrying a bag of groceries, comes in directly behind Darlene.*)

Darlene: "LIAR ON TOP OF EVERYTHING ELSE!"

Mickey: Hi.

Darlene: Hi.

Mickey: How you doing?

Eddie (*Heading for the armchair, where he sits, picking up the newspaper*): Great. You?

Mickey (*Moving to the kitchen, he sets the bag down on the counter, taking out beers*): Terrific. Anybody need a beer?

Eddie: No.

Darlene: Sure. *(Mickey pops open a beer for her and then moves to start up the stairs where he abruptly halts.)*

Mickey: You know what I'm going to do? I'm going to venture a thought that I might regret down the road. And anticipating that regret makes me, you know, hesitate. In the second of hesitation, I get a good look at the real feeling that it is, this regret—a kind of inner blackmail that shows me even further down the road where I would end up having to live with myself as a smaller person, a man less generous to his friends than I would care to be. *(Slowly, carefully, he descends the stairs.)* So, you know, we'll have to put this through a multiprocessing here, but I was outside, I mean, for a while; and what I heard in here was—I mean, it really was passion. Sure, it was a squabble, and anybody could have heard that, but what I heard was more. We all know—everybody knows I'm basically on a goof right now. I'm going back to my wife and kids sooner or later—I don't hide that fact from anybody. And what I really think is that fact was crucial to the development of this whole thing because it made me WHAT? Safe. A viable diversion from what might have actually been a genuine, meaningful, and to that same extent and maybe even more so—threatening—connection between you two. I'm not going to pretend I wasn't up for it, too—but I was never anything but above board. You know—a couple jokes, nice dinner, that's my style. Good wine, we gotta spend the night—and I don't mean to be crass—because the point is maybe we have been made fools of here by our own sophistication, and what am I protecting by not saying something about it, my vanity? Ego? Who needs it? So, I'm out in the yard and I'm thinking, "Here is this terrific guy, this dynamite lady, and they are obviously, definitely hooked up on some powerful, idiosyncratic channel, so what am I doing in the middle?" Am I totally off base here, Eddie, or what? *(He ends huddling with Eddie, who is in the armchair, while Darlene is seated on the swivel chair behind Mickey.)*

Eddie: You're—I mean, obviously you're not TOTALLY. You know that.

Mickey: That's exactly what I'm saying.

Eddie: I mean, from my end of it.

Mickey: For my own well-being, I don't want to serve as the instrument of some neurotic, triangular bullshit being created here between you two. That's the main issue for me. I mean, from my point of view.

Eddie: Right.

Darlene (*Leaning forward, trying to insert herself into their attention*): I mean, I certainly haven't felt right—I mean, good about it, that's—

Mickey (*Whirling toward her*): Everything went so fast.

Darlene: Everything just happened.

Mickey: You met him, you met me.

Darlene: I met Eddie, and then Eddie, you know, introduces me to you.

Eddie: It's too fast.

Darlene: It was fast.

Mickey (*He strides about between them*): Just—What is this, the electronic age? Sure. But we're people, not computers; the whole program cannot be just reprogrammed without some resolution of the initial, you know, thing that started everything. So I'm going to—I don't know what—but go. Somewhere. Out. And you two can just see where it takes you. Go with the flow. I mean, you guys should see yourselves.

Darlene: I'm just—I mean, I don't—weird, weird, weird.

Mickey (*Patting Darlene's hand*): In all honesty, Darlene, you told me this is what you wanted in more ways than I cared to pay attention to. (*Backing for the door, he looks at Eddie.*) And you, you prick, you were obviously madly in love. (*To Darlene.*) Go easy on him. I'll catch you all later.

Eddie: Down the road.

Darlene: Bye.

Mickey: Just remember, Darlene, you made the wrong choice. (*Mickey goes.*)

Eddie (*Pacing toward the door as if in awe of Mickey*): Where the hell did he come up with the . . . I mean, clarity to do that?

Darlene: That wasn't clarity.

Eddie (*Turning toward Darlene, he perches on the couch arm*): No, no, I mean, it wasn't clarity. But he had to HAVE clarity.

Darlene: I don't know what it was. Generosity?

Eddie: Whatever it was, you don't see it very often. I don't expect that from Mickey, I mean, that kind of thing.

Darlene: Who expects that from anybody? We're all so all over the place.

Eddie: Self-absorbed.

Darlene: And distracted. I'm distracted by everything. I mean, I'm almost always distracted, aren't you?

Eddie: Absolutely.

Darlene: Everything is always distracting me from everything else.

Eddie: Everything is very distracting, but what I've really noticed is that mainly, the thing I'm most distracted by is myself. I mean, I'm my own major distraction, trying to get it together, to get my head together, my act together.

Darlene: Our little minds just buzzzzzzzz! What do they think they're doing?

Eddie: However Mickey managed to get through it, though, I know one thing—I'm glad he did.

Darlene: Are you really?

Eddie: I really missed you. It was amazing. That was probably it—he got his clue from the fact that I never shut up about you. I think I was driving him crazy. How do you feel?

Darlene: Great. I think I was, you know, into some form of obsession about you, too, some form of mental loop. I feel scared is what I feel. Good, too. I feel good, but mainly scared.

Eddie: I'm scared.

Darlene: I mean, a year ago, I was a basket case. If we had met a year ago, I wouldn't have had a prayer.

Eddie: Me, too. A year ago, I was nuts. And I still have all kinds of things to think through. Stuff coming up, I have to think it through.

Darlene: Me, too.

Eddie: And by thinking, I don't mean just some ethereal mental thing either, but being with people is part of it, being with you is part of the thinking, that's how I'm doing the thinking, but I just have to go slow, there's a lot of scar tissue.

Darlene: There's no rush, Eddie.

Eddie: I don't want to rush.

Darlene: I don't want to rush.

Eddie: I can't rush. I'll panic. If I rush, I'll panic.

Darlene: We'll just have to keep our hearts open, as best we can.

Eddie: No pressure.

Darlene: And no guilt, okay?

Eddie: No guilt.

Darlene: We don't want any guilt. I mean, I'm going to be out of town a lot. We both have our lives.

Eddie: We just have to keep our options open.

Darlene: And our hearts, okay?

Eddie: I mean, the right attitude. . . .

Darlene: Exactly. If we have the right attitude. . . .

Eddie: Attitude is so important. And by attitude I don't mean just attitude either, but I mean real emotional space.

Darlene: We both need space.

Eddie: And time. We have to have time.

Darlene: Right. So we can just take the time to allow the emotional space for things to grow and work themselves out.

Eddie: So you wanna go fuck?

They kiss and the MUSIC STARTS: Willie Nelson singing "Someone to Watch Over Me."

BLACKOUT

NOTE: It might be that as the scene progresses, they end up on the couch, undressing each other as they conduct their negotiations; or perhaps it is more strictly a negotiation with distance between them. Or perhaps it is a combination so that each time there is a sense of the negotiations being completed so that physical contact can begin—an embrace, a kiss—some bit of outstanding business is then remembered, and one or the other moves away.

SCENE THREE

TIME: Late Afternoon of the next day.

The music, Willie Nelson singing "Someone to Watch Over Me" continues. Donna, moving to the music, crosses, carrying a beer, and turns on the TV, the volume loud. She flops down on the couch, picking up a magazine, while the music and TV are both playing. The door opens and Phil comes in looking disheveled, in a hurry. He starts talking almost immediately, clearly thinking Eddie is around. He carries two six-packs of beer and a grocery bag containing meat and bread for sandwiches and two huge bags of popcorn. In his pocket is a pint of bourbon in a paper bag from which he sips every now and then.

Phil: So this broad is always here, you know what I mean? What is she, a chair? What are you, a goddamn chair? You sit around here and you would let anybody do anything to you, wouldn't you? Whatsamatter with you? Don't you have any self-respect? You're all alike. She is!

Donna: Who you talkin' to?

Phil *(Yelling up the stairs toward Eddie's room)*: She's got the god-damn TV on and the record player on! Who you workin' for, the electric company? *(He turns off the record player.)*

Donna: Who you talkin' to, Phil?

Phil: Don't call me Phil, okay. Just don't. I'm talkin' to you. Who asked you anyway?

Donna: You ain't talkin' to me, I could tell by your tone. Who you talkin' to?

Phil: You're very observant. You're very smart. Who was I talkin' to?

Donna: I don't know. I'm the only one here.

Phil: I was talkin' to Eddie.

Donna: Eddie ain't here.

Phil: He's up in his room.

Donna: He ain't.

Phil *(Running up the stairs to look into the bathroom and then Eddie's room)*: EDDIE! EDDIE! Where the hell are you? *(Stepping out of Eddie's room.)* I was just talkin' to him.

Donna: That's what I been trying to explain to you.

Phil *(Leaning over the railing to yell down to her)*: Get off my back, will you? You dumb bitch. Get off it. You're on me all the time.

Donna: I ain't.

Phil *(Heading toward Mickey's room, he opens the door and looks in)*: The fuck you ain't.

Donna: I'm sorry. I'm just sittin' here.

Phil: Like hell you are.

Donna: I'm sorry.

Phil *(Coming down the stairs)*: You oughta be sorry. You're a sorry goddamn piece of just whatever the hell you are.

Donna: Am I botherin' you? I am just sitting here.

Phil: With your head up your ass.

Donna: I was readin' a magazine.

Phil: With your head up your ass.

Donna: Boy, you are really an insulting form of person. Honest to god. Let a person have some rest. *(On his way to the kitchen, Phil freezes and then whirls to face her.)*

Phil: Meaning me?

Donna: Whata you mean?

Phil: I mean, "meanin' me?" Who's SOMETHIN'?

Donna: I didn't mean nothin'. I never mean nothin'.

Phil: You said it though, didn't you?

Donna: What?

Phil: What you said? You fuckin' said it.

Donna: I don't know what you're talkin' about. Exactly.

Phil *(Heading into the kitchen where he starts to pour the popcorn in a bowl and tries to make sandwiches)*: What I'm talkin' about is how you are and what you said. You see a guy has undergone certain difficulties so his whole appearance thing is a mood thing of how he is obviously in a discouraged state, he's full of turmoil, does it occur to you to say a kindly thing or to cut his fuckin' heart out? You got your tongue out to sharpen your knife is what you're up to, or do you want to give me some other explanation?

Donna: Sure, because—

Phil: So what is it?

Donna: What?

Phil: Your so-called explanation! Let's hear it.

Donna: I'm just—

Phil: Bullshit. Bull Shit!

Donna: No.

Phil (*As Eddie comes in the front door with a bag of pretzels and clothes from the cleaners*): Would you listen to this air head?

Eddie: How's everything?

Phil: Terrific. It's all totally fucked up, which I wouldn't have it any other way. I thought you was here.

Eddie: I hadda go out.

Phil (*Moving toward Eddie*): Your car was here. What the fuck is going on?

Eddie: It wasn't far, so I walked. Donna, hey, I thought you were on your way to—

Phil: Listen, Eddie! I saw the car, I thought you were here, you know, I was talkin' to you, you wasn't here, so I sounded like this asshole, so the ditz here has got to get on me about it.

Eddie: Don't fuck with Phil, Donna.

Donna: I wasn't, Eddie.

Eddie: I mean, did you bring her, Phil?

Phil: Who?

Donna: No, no, no.

Eddie: She's here ain't she!

Donna: I was hitchhiking, Eddie, and it was like he come outa nowhere and it was, wow, Mickey. Whata hot car. So I set out for San Francisco like we talked about but I ended up here.

Phil: I mean, what is it with this goddamn broad that makes her tick? I wanna know what makes her fuckin' tick. You answer me that goddamn question, will you?

Donna: What?

Phil: What makes you tick? I come here to see Eddie, you gotta be here. I wanna watch the football game and talk over some very important issues which pertain to my life, you gotta be here. What the fuck makes you tick?

Donna: What's he talkin' about?

Eddie: I don't know.

Phil: What I'm talkin' about is—

Eddie: Listen, Phil, if Darlene comes by, you just introduce Donna as your ditz, okay? *(He starts up the stairs for his room.)*

Phil: What?

Eddie: You found her, you know. Darlene's gonna be by at any second, we're goin' to the desert for the weekend. Can you do that? *(As he goes running into his room.)*

Donna: Who's Darlene, Phil?

Phil *(Crossing to get some of his food)*: I'm beggin' you. I'm beggin' you. I don't wanna see you, okay? I don't wanna see you.

Donna: Okay.

Phil: I mean, I come in here and you gotta be here; I'm thinkin' about football, and you gotta be here with your tits and your ass and this tight shrunken clothes and these shriveled jeans, so that's all I'm thinking about from the minute I see you is tits and ass. Football doesn't have a chance against it. It's like this invasion of tits and ass overwhelming my own measly individuality so I don't have a prayer to have my own thoughts about my own things except you and tits and ass and sucking and fucking and that's all I can think about. My privacy has been demolished. You think a person wants to have that kind of thing happen to their heads—they are trying to give their own problems some serious thought, the next thing they know there's nothing in their brains as far as they can see but your tits and ass? You think a person likes that?

Donna: Who's playin'?

Phil: You think a person likes that?

Donna: No.

Phil: Who's playin' what?

Donna: Football.

Phil: None of your fuckin' business.

Donna: I like it.

Phil: What are you talkin' about? I don't know what you're talkin' about.

Donna: Football.

Phil: You're nuts.

Donna: I wanna watch it with you.

Phil: You're nuts! You wanna watch the game? You're talkin' about you wanna watch the football game? Are you nuts? Are you crazy?

Donna: What?

Phil: How you gonna watch it? You don't know about it. You don't know nothing about it.

Donna: I do. I know the points, and the insignias, and the—

Phil: That's not the game.

Donna: And when they go through the air and they catch it.

Phil: Get outta here. I don't want you here.

Donna: I know about the mascots.

Phil: You wanna know about the game? You wanna know about it? *(He has moved to grab her head between his two hands.)* You don't know about the fucking game. Hut, hut, hut—

Donna: What are you doin'? What are you—*(He butts his head into hers.)*

Phil: That's the game. That's the game.

Donna: Ohh, ouch ouch, awwwww owwwwww. *(Eddie comes out of his bedroom, a bunch of clothes in his hands.)*

Eddie: What's this now?

Phil: She's cryin'. What the fuck is the matter with her?

Donna: He hit me, he hit me.

Phil: She says she wants to know about the game.

Eddie: What game?

Donna: Football—

Phil: —football!

Donna: That's all.

Phil: She's nuts.

Donna: He hurt me. Am I bleedin'? Eddie, Eddie, Eddie.

Eddie: No.

Donna *(Running to the record player, grabbing the record)*: This is shit, this is shit. This is shit.

Eddie: What happened?

Phil: I don't know. It was over too fast.

Eddie: What? *(Donna is running up the stairs now.)*

Phil: This thing here, whatever it was that happened here. She wanted to know about football, you know, the crazy bitch. She can't know about football. It's impossible. It's totally one hundred percent impossible. So this is what happens. *(Going into the bathroom, Donna slams the door.)* So how you doin'?

Eddie: Great. Me and Darlene are goin' to the desert.

Phil: So guess what?

Eddie *(He disappears back into his room)*: What?

Phil *(Heading up the stairs)*: It's almost decided. I'm almost decided about going back to Susie.

Eddie *(From off)*: What?

Phil *(Hovering outside Eddie's room)*: I can't stand it. The loneliness. And some form of totally unusual and unpredictable insanity is creeping up on me about to do I don't know WHAT— God forbid I find out. So I been thinkin' maybe if we had the kid, everything, or at least the main things, might be okay.

Eddie *(Coming out of his bedroom)*: What kid?

Phil: We were tryin' to have a kid. That's what we been doin'.

Eddie: You and Susie?

Phil: Eddie, wake up here! Who you think? Yeah, me and Susie. She wants a kid. All her friends have been havin' 'em.

Eddie *(As he backs along the balcony toward the bathroom door)*: It's that goddamn age where it hits 'em like a truck, this maternal urge; they gotta have a kid—they don't know what hit 'em. *(Eddie knocks on the bathroom door.)*

Phil: So it hit Susie; but maybe it's what I need, you know.

Eddie: Were you doin' that insanity with the thermometer and, you know, you gotta fuck on schedule?

Phil: Unbelievable!

Eddie: Because that stuff is insanity. *(And again Eddie knocks on the bathroom door, which opens, and Donna comes out, walking straight to Mickey's room.)*

Phil: The trouble is though, what if it doesn't work out the way I planned it?

Eddie: Nothin' does, Phil. *(He steps into the bathroom, and Phil comes around to stand looking in at Eddie.)*

Phil: I mean, I wanna have a kid sometimes, and sometimes I'm scared to death, and mostly though, I mean, for the last month or so it was like in my thoughts in my mind sometimes this little baby had this big gun to my head and she would shoot me sooner or later.

Eddie *(As Eddie comes out of the bathroom, zipping up a shaving kit, and heading for his room)*: So you don't want a kid.

Phil: I do and I don't. I do and I don't.

Eddie *(Pausing on the balcony, he faces Phil)*: I think this might be the thing here, you know, about which you two have been fighting so much lately. You shouldn't probably have one now. Just go back and get some, you know, clarity, so you both know what the issues are. This is the relationship I'm talkin' about. Straighten that out.

Phil: Right. And then see. That makes sense.

Eddie: Sure. *(Eddie steps into his room.)*

Phil: Except she has to have one.

Eddie *(Coming out of his room, carrying a small suitcase, the shaving kit, and a garment bag)*: She don't have to have one.

Phil *(Following Eddie as they descend the stairs)*: I tried tellin' her that, because you know I got three kids, two little boys and a girl who are now, you know, I don't know how old, in Toledo, I haven't seen 'em since I went to prison. I don't want any more kids out there, you know, rollin' around their beds at night with this sick fucking hatred of me. I can't stand it.

Eddie: Who could stand it?

Phil: Right.

Eddie: So don't have the kid now.

Phil: Right. *(As Eddie, at the kitchen counter grabs his dope box in order to pack it.)* Except she's desperate. I can't stand it when she cries.

Eddie: You can't stand it when she cries is no reason to have a kid, Phil. I mean, a kid is a big fuckin' gamble.

Phil: Hey, as we both well know, Eddie, what isn't a gamble? You're alive, you gamble!

Eddie: Yeh, but the collateral here is, you know, this other person you can't even ask what they think of the odds. There is involved here an innocent helpless person totally dependent on your good will.

Phil: It's fuckin' depressing. How about some weed? I want some weed.

Eddie: What I'm sayin', Phil, is first things first.

Phil: Like what?

Eddie: The marriage; the marriage. *(Giving a joint to Phil, Eddie lights it for him and gives Phil complete attention now at the kitchen counter.)* I mean, no kid and a divorce is who-gives-a-fuck, but you have a kid and it's seismic. A big ten on the Richter scale.

Carnage, man, that's what I'm sayin', gore on the highway. Add in the kid and it's a major disaster.

Phil (*Passing the lit joint to Eddie, Phil sits on the swivel chair outside the counter*): Right. Sure. Except, see, the trouble is, Susie has wanted to be a mother since she was twelve, you know. She had dolls and teddy bears and she dressed them up in diapers—you know—she still does it, sometimes. It was all she ever dreamed about.

Eddie: Still does what?

Phil: I wanna make her happy, Eddie. I mean, if she's happy, maybe I'll be happy. So she's got teddy bears, so what.

Eddie (*Sitting opposite Phil*): I mean, you're not thinkin' of going back and just, you know, hoping for the best; I mean, just trusting it to luck that she won't get pregnant. You're not thinkin' that.

Phil: No, fuck, no.

Eddie: Because you won't have a chance if you're sayin' that, and you go back.

Phil: I got it covered, Eddie.

Eddie: She'll eat you alive.

Phil: I got it covered, Eddie, is what I'm sayin'. I got the situation totally covered. There's nothin' to worry about on that score. I been takin' this stuff and messing the whole thing up, which is why we ain't pregnant at this very minute.

Eddie: Whata you mean?

Phil: You know, my sperm count is monstrous on its own.

Eddie: Whata you mean?

Phil: I have a very high sperm count. It's record setting.

Eddie: What stuff?

Phil: Stuff. You know, it's harmful to the sperm and I'm messing myself up.

Eddie: You're taking some kind of—Wait a minute! You're telling me you're taking some kind of poison?

Phil: That's why I hadda talk to you, Eddie.

Eddie: Do you know what the hell you're saying to me?

Phil: What?

Eddie (*Leaping to his feet, Eddie marches to the clothes from the cleaners*): This is insane! You're taking some kind of goddamn poison because—This is crazy, Phil! This is nuts! It's fucking nuts!

Phil: It's not poison.

Eddie (*Ripping open the paper wrapped around the box containing the shirts*): Listen to me. Do me a favor. Tell her what's been going on. You can tell her, can't you?

Phil: Sure.

Eddie (*Putting shirts into the suitcase*): So do it. If you're going back, you gotta do it. She's your wife, for god's sake, you can talk to her.

Phil: Sure.

Eddie: So explain the situation to her. (*Grabbing the dope box, he starts to go with it to put it in the suitcase.*) I mean, don't you think maybe this is why the hell you two been fighting?

Phil: Are you mad at me?

Eddie: No.

Phil: You're sure.

Eddie: I'm just excited. Sometimes I get like I'm angry when I get excited. (*He is putting the sport jacket and trousers from the cleaners in the clothing bag.*)

Phil: Right. Because you are absolutely without a doubt one hundred percent right in everything you're saying, but if I don't do it, what's gonna happen?

Eddie: You gotta do it.

Phil: She gets so sad. Eddie, she gets so goddamn sad, I can't stand it.

Eddie: But it'll be worse if you have the kid—it'll just all be a million zillion times worse. You know that. That's what we've been talking about here.

Phil: Without a doubt. And I'm going to do it, I just want to know what kind of latitude I have regarding our friendship if my mind gets changed.

Eddie: Listen to me—are you a deaf man? Am I only under the delusion that I'm speaking? What you're telling me is a horror story—one part of you is begging another part to stop, but you don't hear you. But I do, I hear—you have got to stop, Phil.

Phil: I know this, Eddie. But what if I can't? Give me some sort of hint regarding your reaction, so I know.

Eddie: What'd she do, hypnotize you? Is this voodoo? You're a grown man. You have asked me to tell you. I'm telling you: "Tell her!"

Phil: You're not answering my question. I'm talking about our friendship here!

Eddie: You're switching the goddamn subject is what you're doing.

Phil: What the hell are you talking about? Why are you avoiding my question?

Eddie: Our friendship doesn't matter here. Our friendship is totally, categorically, one hundred percent irrelevant here.

Phil: Eddie, listen to yourself! This is our friendship—this conversation—these very exchanges. We are in our friendship. What could be more important?

Eddie: I mean, I don't feel . . . What?

Phil: Scorn. You feel scorn for me.

Eddie: No.

Phil: It's in your eyes.

Eddie: No. What? *(He unzips the shaving kit to get out a container of Alka Seltzer.)*

Phil: These dark thoughts, Eddie, I see them reflected in your eyes, they pertain to something other than me, or what?

Eddie: I'm not having dark thoughts.

Phil: Beyond the thoughts you're thinking, Eddie.

Eddie *(Crossing to the sink for water)*: No!

Phil: Then what the hell are you thinking about? I come for advice and you're off on some other totally unrelated tangent, is that the thing here, the goddamn bottom line? I need your attention, and you're off in some fucking daydream? I'm desperate and you are, for crissake, distracted? Is this friendship, Eddie? Tell me!

Eddie: Wait a minute.

Phil: You want a fucking minute?

Eddie: I don't know what you're talking about. *(He drops the tablets in a glass of water.)*

Phil *(Trying to be helpful, to explain)*: Dark thoughts. Your dark thoughts, Eddie. This is not uncommon for people to have them. You were provoked; think nothing of it. But please—this, now—dark thoughts and everything included, this is our friendship. Pay attention to it, it's slipping by.

Eddie: Right! Yeh! I wanna!

Phil *(Patiently explaining)*: I mean, if I do something you consider foolhardy, you won't just dismiss my feelings and my effort and the fact that I came to you.

Eddie: I feel like you're drillin' little fuckin' chunks of cottage cheese into my brain. I'm gettin' confused here, Phil, I tol' you, I don't feel good. *(He is moving, almost staggering toward the couch.)*

Phil *(Following along, puffing a joint)*: It's chaotic is why you're confused, Eddie. That's why you're confused. Think nothin' of it. I'm confused. The goddamn situation is like this masked fucking robber come to steal the goods, but we don't even know is he, or isn't he. I mean, we got these dark thoughts, I see 'em in you, you don't think you're thinkin' 'em, so we can't even nail that down, how we going to get beyond it? They are the results of your unnoticed inner goings-on or my gigantic paranoia, both of which exist, so the goddamn thing in its entirety is on the basis of what has got to be called a coin toss.

Eddie: I can figure it, I can—It's not a goddamn coin toss!

Phil: You think I'm being cynical when I say that? Nothing is necessary, Eddie. Not a fucking thing! We're in the hands of something, it could kill us now or later, it don't care. Who is this guy that makes us just—you know—WHAT? THERE'S A NAME FOR THIS—IT HAPPENS—THERE'S A WORD FOR IT—EVERYBODY KNOWS IT, I CAN'T THINK OF IT. IT'S LIKE A LAW. IT IS A LAW. WHAT'S A LAW? WHAT THE FUCK IS A LAW? Cynicism has nothing to do with it, Eddie, I've done my best. The fucking thing is without a clue, except the mess it leaves behind it, the guts and gore. What I'm sayin' is, if my conclusion is contrary to your wishes, at least give me the fucking consideration and respect that you know that at least from my point of view it is based on solid thought and rock hard evidence that has led me to I have no other choice, so you got no right to fuck with me about it. I want your respect, Eddie. *(He ends leaning intently toward Eddie on the couch.)*

Eddie: You got that, Phil.

Phil: I do?

Eddie: Don't you know that? I'm just sayin'—all I'm sayin' is, "Don't have the baby thoughtlessly."

Phil: Eddie, for god sake, don't terrify me that you have paid no attention! If I was thoughtless would I be here? I feel like I have pushed thought to the brink where it is just noise and of no more use than a headful of car horns, because the bottom line here that I'm getting at is just this—I got to go back to her. I got to go back to Susie, and if it means havin' a kid, I got to do it. I mean, I have hit a point where I am going round the bend several times a day now, and so far I been on the other side to meet me, but one a these days it might be one time too many, and who knows who might be there waitin'? If not me, who? I'm a person, Eddie, and I have realized it, who needs like a big-dot-thing, you know—this big-dot-thing around which I can just hang and blab my thoughts and more or less formulate everything as I go, myself included. I mean, I used to spend my days in my car; I didn't know what the fuck I was doin' but it kept me out of trouble until nothin' but blind luck led me to I-am-married, and I could go home. She was my big-dot-thing. Now I'm startin' in my car again, I'm spendin' days on the freeways and rain or no rain I like the wipers clickin', and all around me the other cars got people in 'em the way I see them when they are in cars. These heads, these faces. These boxes of steel with glass and faces inside. I been the last three days without seeing another form of human being in his entirety except gas station attendants. The family men in the day with their regular food and regular hours in their eyes. And then in the night, these moonlighters; they could be anything. In the wee hours of the morning, it's derelicts, and these weird spooky kids like they have recently arrived from outer space, but not to stay. The cloverleafs, they got a thing in them, it spins me off. There's little back roads and little towns sometimes I never heard of them. I start to expect the gas station attendants to know me when I arrive. I get excited that I've been there before. I want them to welcome me. I'm disappointed when they don't. Something that I don't want to be true starts lookin' like it's all that's true only I don't know what it is. No. No. I need my marriage. I come here to tell you. I got to stay married. I'm lost without her.

The door to Mickey's room slams loudly as out comes Donna. She is dressed in shorts far too snug for her, and a tight T-shirt shortened above her belly button, and she carries her record and other belongings.

Donna (*At the top of the stairs*): You guys have cooked your goose. You can just walk your own dog, and fuck yourselves. These particular tits and ass are taking a hike. (*She stomps down the stairs and struts to the door, opens it, turns, looks at Eddie who is staring at her, quite ill.*) So this is goodbye. (*She goes out, slamming the door.*)

CURTAIN

Act Two

SCENE ONE

TIME: Night. A year later.

PLACE: The same.

Eddie lies on the floor, nestled on pillows, while Mickey is seated, legs dangling through the spokes of the second floor railing. Each has a drink. Phil and Artie are a twosome, a kind of team, standing and drinking, both involved with one another and their memory of the event in which they recently participated and which they are trying to communicate to Mickey and Eddie. Phil has ice wrapped in a towel around his right hand. Artie is so proud of Phil you would think he had himself performed the deed they are excitedly relating. At the breakfast nook, he pours drinks for himself and Phil.

Phil: This guy, what a fuckin' guy.

Artie: You shoulda seen him. He was unbelievable.

Eddie: So what happened?

Phil: I decked him; he deserved it.

Eddie: So what happened?

Phil: He made me mad.

Artie: He was a jerk.

Eddie: So you decked this guy.

Artie (*Rushing near to Phil, hugging him, patting him*): You shoulda seen it. The guy went across the room. He looked like he was on wheels.

Eddie: So what'd he do?

Phil: He got up.

Artie: The dumb fuck.

Eddie: I mean, why'd you hit him?

Phil: He got up!

Eddie (*Sitting up, trying to make his point*): I mean, before he got knocked down—the first time you hit him, why'd you hit him?

Artie: You wouldn't believe this guy. He was genuinely irritating.

Phil: This is the pitiful part. I don't think he could help himself.

Artie: I mean, this is the way this pathetic jerk-off must go through his life. IRRITATING!

Phil: It's a curse to be this guy! I shoulda had some consideration.

Eddie (*Going to the kitchen*): BUT WHAT HAPPENED?

Artie: He was sayin' this unbelievable dumb stuff to this broad.

Eddie (*In the kitchen Eddie pours another drink*): Some broad you knew?

Artie: Noooo! (*As if this is the dumbest question anybody ever could have asked.*) Just this genuinely repulsive broad.

Phil: And he's talkin' to her like she's somethin' gorgeous. THIS DOG! It was offensive. Who'd he think he was with, you know? This was nobody of any even remotely dynamite qualities, you know what I mean? You don't talk to some dog in the manner he's talking. It's disgusting!

Artie: Very irritating guy.

Eddie: I can see that.

Phil: You shoulda been there. I ask him to shut up, and he says he isn't botherin' anybody. I says he is botherin' me; he looks at me like I'm an asshole; I can see he's askin' for it, so I warn him one more time.

Eddie: What'd you say?

Phil: I don't SAY nothing. I look at him very seriously, you know, bullets and razors and bloodshed in my eyes, but all under control, so he can have the option of knowing nothing need happen if he don't push me. But he's gotta push me.

Mickey: So what happened?

Phil: It all went very quickly—

Artie: —the guy goes right off the stool!

Eddie *(With his drink, Eddie leans intently in toward Phil, exasperated, yet playing at the exasperation, enjoying the fact that they cannot seem to make any sense to one another)*: But what happened?

Artie: He got up.

Eddie: He got up?

Mickey: He got up? This is unbelievable. You knock him down, he gets up?

Artie: Phil don't just knock him down. He knocks him across the room. *(And now Artie in order to demonstrate, runs crashing backwards into a wall.)* It's like this goddamn vortex just snarfs him up and fucking magnetizes him to the wall for a full second before he slides to the floor. SO THEN HE GETS UP! Do you believe this guy?

Phil: Personally, this is where the guy gets a raw deal, though, 'cause the second time I was wired into some other frequency, and the whack I put on him was beyond the realm of normal human punches. That he didn't disintegrate was both his and my good fortune.

Mickey: This is some tough guy, huh?

Artie and Phil: NOOOOO! NOOOO! *(As if this is an insanely stupid question.)*

Phil: Absolutely not. This is a weak link on the chain of humanity other than in his particular capacities of irritating; and this is where the real irony comes in. Because I don't think, looking back, that when he got up on his feet again he any longer had a clue to where he was or what he was doin'.

Artie: He was totally fuckin' unconscious.

Phil: Exactly. Looking back, I can see he was no longer from his point of view in the bar even. From his point of view he was on his way to catch a bus or something.

Artie: It was his reflexes.

Phil: Exactly, but I don't see he's harmless in time to take charge of my own reflexes, which see nothing at all except that he's comin' toward me. So I gotta let him have it. It's him or me.

Artie: But as far as attacking Phil, it's the farthest thing from his mind.

Phil: No, he's like going shopping or something. He don't know what he's doing. It's just his reflexes.

Artie: His reflexes got the best of him.

Phil: So we are both victims of our reflexes.

Mickey (*Pronouncing from where he sits on high*): So, this is a tragedy here.

Phil: I don't know about that, but it was a mess, and I coulda got into real trouble, because the force with which I hit him is even in my memory of it nerve-wracking.

Artie: Don't get morose, Phil, huh? (*Patting Phil, trying to cheer him up.*) Pay attention to the upside.

Phil: You pay attention to the upside—you're the big deal— I'm the fuck-up. (*Pulling away from Artie, Phil moves over to the TV where he has spied a vial of coke.*)

Eddie (*Following after Phil*): You let off some steam, Phil. This is the purpose of this kind of, you know, out and out bullshit.

Phil (*Picking up the coke*): You wanna tell me how come I have all the necessary realizations that any normal human being might have—only I have them too late, so that I understand he's a pathetic, unconscious jerk-off who can't help irritating people and is oblivious to the fact that he is on his feet—only by the time I understand it, he's unconscious and nothing but luck has kept me from doing a lifetime in the can; so the realizations can serve no possible useful purpose on earth but to torment me with the thought that I am a merciless, totally out of control prick. Whata you wanna call that? I call it horseshit.

Artie: Phil has got violent karma, that's all; it's in the cards. *(Behind the breakfast nook counter he has a notebook in which he starts to scribble.)*

Phil: Yeh, well, I am running out of patience with being good for nothing but whacking people in the face they do some irrelevant thing that drives me nuts. If this is my karma, to be an asshole and have such a thing as this, fuck it.

Mickey *(Rising languidly to his feet)*: Absolutely, right; fuck destiny, fate and all metaphysical stuff.

Phil *(Bolting to the base of the stairway where he glares up at Mickey)*: You, you cynical bastard, watch the fine line you are walking between my self-awareness and my habitual trend to violence. 'Cause on the one hand I might appear worried, but on the other I could give a fuck, you know, and my urge to annihilate anyone might just fixate on you.

Mickey *(Descending the stairs toward a bottle of Scotch by the TV)*: And the vortex get me—fling me, you might say, wallward, magnetically.

Phil: Exactly. So you can help us both out by watching your goddamn, you know—right? Am I making myself clear?

Mickey *(Slipping by Phil)*: Step.

Phil: Yeah. P's and Q's. *(Moving after Mickey, but yelling to Artie who is busy scribbling at the breakfast nook.)* So, Artie, you got any inside dope on this karma thing, or you just ranting?

Artie: Everybody knows something, it's a popular topic.

Phil *(Turning to Artie)*: But what I'm asking you is, "You said it, do you know it?"

Eddie *(Moving near Phil)*: I mean, Phil, isn't the fact of the matter here that you signed your divorce papers today?

Phil: Who said anything about that? One thing does not lead to another.

Eddie: I mean, I think that's what you're wired up about.

Phil: Eddie, you're jumpin' around on me, here, what's your point?

Eddie: The baby, the baby. The divorce. This is the ambush you been worried about. They got you. They blew you the fuck right out of orbit, and if you see maybe that's what's cooking under the whole thing, you might just get a hold of yourself.

Mickey: And pull yourself back into orbit.

Phil: But what orbit? I'm in an orbit.

Mickey: It's just it's a useless fucking orbit.

Phil (*Crossing slowly to Mickey*): Do you know, Mickey, I could kick your eyes out and never think about it a second time, that's the depths to which my animosity runs?!

Mickey: I know that.

Phil: So why do you take these chances and risk ruining both our lives?

Mickey: This is the very point Artie was, I think, making.

Phil: Artie, is this your point? (*Turning, looking for Artie.*)

Artie: What? (*Unnoticed by the others, Artie has settled down in the corner on a pile of pillows and he does not even look up from his scribbling, as Phil comes rushing toward him.*)

Phil: Is this your point?

Artie: What?

Eddie (*Moving in on Mickey*): Mickey! Will you just cut the goofy shit for a second? This is a serious point I'm trying to make here.

Mickey: He knows his life is a mess.

Eddie: He doesn't know it enough.

Mickey: He knows it so goddamn well he's trying to avoid it.

Eddie: That's my point! I mean, Phil, if you see the goddamn issue here. PHIL!

Phil (*Looking up from Artie's endeavor*): YEAH. What's Artie doin'?

Artie: I had a thought.

Phil: So you wrote it down? Everybody has a thought, Artie, this is no justification they go around writing them down.

Eddie (*Approaching Phil, trying to force his attention*): You're just on a goddamn wild roll here because of the state of your life being a shambles! The baby's born and you sign the divorce papers all in the same month, so you're under stress.

Phil: I'm aware of that.

Eddie: So that's what I'm sayin'. See the connection.

Phil: But why are you trying to torment me, Eddie? I thought I could count on you.

Eddie: But lighten up is what I'm saying. Give yourself a break. I mean, the real issues are not you hitting people or not hitting people, but are these other issues of your divorce and baby. You enjoy hitting people and you know it.

Phil: My point is not that I don't enjoy it but that it is dangerous, and mostly dangerous that I do enjoy it, so what's the point in that? And my point is that I am wired beyond my reasons. I know my reasons, but I am wired beyond them.

Mickey (*Moving near, his manner a seeming friendliness*): You're right on schedule, Phil, that's all. You're a perfectly, rapateta, blah-blah-blah, modern statistic; you have the baby, you get the divorce. You're very "now" is all, but not up to it. You're the definitive representative of the modern male in this year, but you're not willing to accept it.

Phil (*Undergoing an impulse to throw Mickey through a wall*): This is what I gotta talk to Artie about. (*He turns and finds Artie at the breakfast nook, picking up the phone.*) Artie, what the fuck are you doing?

Artie: I'm checking my messages.

Phil (*Hurrying to Artie*): You got a minute, this is a disaster here. I'm on the brink and you're checking your fucking messages. Have some compassion. (*He is trying to get Artie to hang up.*)

Artie: Just a second. (*He beeps his beeper into the phone.*)

Eddie: So who'd you hear from, huh? You got studio executives lined up on your goddamn machine beep after beep. *(Mimicking different voices.)* "Great project, Arthur." "Terrific treatment." "Must have lunch."

Artie: I have a career. I am not ashamed, I have a career. You want me to be ashamed?

Eddie: What I want you to understand, Artie, is the absurdity of this business, and the fact that you're a success in it is a measure of the goddamn absurdity of this business to which we are all desperate to belong as a bunch of dogs.

Artie: You're a small-minded prick, Eddie; I hope you know that.

Mickey *(Having settled down on the window seat)*: He does.

Eddie: I am familiar with the opinion. However, I do not myself hold it.

Phil *(Unable to wait any longer, he grabs at the phone, but Artie eludes him, determined to get his messages)*: But what I need, Artie, is a little more, you know what I mean, Artie. What I'm wondering here is, you got any particularly useful, I mean, hard data on this karma stuff, you know, the procedures by which this cosmic shit comes down. That's what I'm asking: Do you know what you're talking about?

Mickey: He's a Jew.

Phil: I know he's a Jew. I'm talking to him, ain't I? Destiny is a thing you have to be somewhat educated to have a hint about it, so he might know somebody, right, Artie? You know anybody?

Eddie: But it's another tradition, Phil.

Phil: Who gives a fuck!? Of course I know that. But I'm not talking about tradition here—I'm asking him about the cosmos and has he come upon anything in all the fucking books he reads that might tell me more than I pick up off the TV which is, strictly speaking, dip-shit.

Artie *(Behind Phil, hanging up the phone)*: Sure.

Phil: See. So what is it?

Artie: Hey, you know, past lives, you have past lives and the karmic stuff accrues to it. You have debts and credits and you have to work your way out from under the whole thing, so you—

Mickey: Artie! This is not your investment counselor we're talking about here.

Eddie: This is not cosmic Visa, Artie.

(Mickey and Eddie are both laughing now—Mickey, wanting fun and to keep Phil from being taken seriously by anyone, and Eddie because he is irritated that Phil seems more interested in Artie's opinions than in the advice Eddie himself has tried to give.)

Artie: We could be in the process of working out the debits and credits of our past lives with the very way we relate to each other at this very instant. It could be that Phil owes some affection to me, I owe him some guidance, and—

Eddie *(Laughing even more now. Mickey and Eddie both breaking up)*: Guidance?

Mickey: The fact that you're talking, Artie, does not necessarily make it destiny speaking, I hope you know this.

Artie: And you two pricks owe some negative shit to everybody.

Phil: Artie, he's right. You make it sound like the cosmos is in your opinion this loan shark. This is disappointing.

Artie: You asked me.

Phil: Because I thought you might know.

Mickey: That's the TV fucking version, and don't you pretend you learned that anywhere but on the evening news.

Eddie: Some goddamn Special Project.

Phil: I was hoping, you know, he's a Jew. He's got this insane religious history running out behind him, he might have picked up something, you know. That's what I was hoping. There might be some crazed Hasidic motherfucker in his family; you know, he came to dinner, he had his pigtail, nobody could shut him up about karma, destiny, the way of the stars; it might have rubbed off on Artie.

Mickey: You disappointed him, Artie. You built him up, you disappointed him.

Artie: It happens.

Mickey: He's at a critical juncture in his life, here.

Artie: Who isn't?

Eddie: You guys need to get laid.

Mickey: You, however, don't, huh?

Eddie: I am, in fact, sustaining a meaningful relationship.

Artie (*Irritated that Eddie and Mickey have teased him, he thinks he will tease back, snapping out his real feelings*): The only thing sustaining that relationship is the fact that she's out of town two out of every three weeks.

Eddie (*Glaring at Artie*): Well, she's in town tomorrow.

Mickey (*After an uneasy second*): I wouldn't mind getting laid. What are we thinking about?

Eddie: We could call somebody.

Phil: Do it.

Artie: Do it now!

Eddie: I was thinking primarily of setting Phil up, that's what I meant, primarily.

Artie: What about me?

Eddie: Give me a break, Artie. Phil is in a totally unique situation, here, back out in the single life.

Phil: I'm in a totally fucked-up state of mind, too.

Artie: I mean, that little blonde might still be around, you hadn't decided to beat the shit out of her.

Phil: Is everything my fault, Artie? I mean, relent, I beg you, I am feeling suicidal. Haven't I explained myself?

Artie: She liked us. She would have stayed a long time.

Phil: I was teaching her football. It was an accident. I went too far.

Eddie: So I could call Bonnie.

Artie: You're not going to get Bonnie for Phil?

Phil: I don't believe this treachery. Artie, have some mercy.

Phil and Artie spin off into their own little squabble, Phil pushing at Artie, trying to shut him up, while Eddie goes to the phone to start dialing and Mickey watches them all.

Artie: This is sex we're talking about now, Phil. Competitive sex.

Phil: That's what I'm saying. I need help.

Artie: You're such a jerk-off, you're such a goof-off. I don't believe for a second you were seriously desperate about trying to pick that bitch up.

Phil: That's exactly how out of touch I am, Artie—I have methods so out-dated they appear to you a goof.

Artie *(Artie runs toward Mickey, Phil chasing playfully after him)*: Fuck you. He's got this thing.

Phil: Styles have changed. Did you see the look of disgust on that bimbo's excuse for a face? It was humiliating.

Artie *(Trying to tell Mickey)*: He's got this thing!

Phil: It used to work. *(Pulling Artie away from Mickey, Phil throws him toward the couch, where the two of them collapse, giggling.)*

Mickey: What thing? *(Eddie is at the phone, dialing.)*

Phil: It's a vibrator that I carry around, see.

Mickey: You carry around a vibrator with you?

Phil: As a form of come-on, so they see I'm up for anything right from the get-go. It's very logical if you think about it. But tonight there were extenuating circumstances.

Artie: It's a logic apparent to you alone, Phil.

Eddie *(Slamming down the phone)*: Bonnie, get off the fucking phone!

Mickey: He had a vibrator.

Phil: I had a vibrator. So what?

Eddie: It's logical.

Phil: Right. Eddie understands me, thank god for it. So when I'm coming on to the broad, see, I sort of pull it out, and have it there. It's like some other guy might have a nail file or something only I got a vibrator—so this Bonnie's a terrific broad, huh?

Eddie: Terrific.

Artie: So you got your thing.

Phil: So I'm delivering my pitch, you know, and we can have a good time if we get an opportunity to be alone, and as a kind of mood-setter, I turn it on, you know. Except I forgot about the goddamn weights.

Eddie: What?

Mickey: THE WEIGHTS? YOU FORGOT ABOUT THE WEIGHTS?

Phil: I forgot about 'em. Unbelievable!

Mickey: UNBELIEVABLE! YOU FORGOT ABOUT THE WEIGHTS! *(To Eddie across the room.)* HE FORGOT ABOUT THE GODDAMN WEIGHTS!

Artie: Do you know what he's talking about?

Mickey: No, I don't know what he's talking about!

Phil: You prick. You disgust me. I'm talking about the weights.

Artie: See, he has been transporting his barbells and weights in the back of the car, with all his inability to know where he lived.

Phil: So the weights were in the back of the car.

Mickey: Right.

Phil: The train of events in this thing is perfectly logical to anybody with half a heart to see them, unless that person is a nasty prick. So what had to happen, happened, and I threw the weights into the trunk of the car carelessly and hit the vibrator without thinking about it.

Eddie: So you pulled out a broken vibrator on this broad.

Phil: Exactly.

Eddie: This is an emergency. I think this is an emergency situation here. *(Whirling back to the phone he begins furiously dialing.)*

Phil: This is what I'm trying to tell you.

Eddie: You're a desperate human being, Phil.

Phil: I'm begging. Get Bonnie! I got this broken vibrator, and so when I turn it on, it goes round sort of all weird like, you know, and the motor's demented sounding, it's going around all crooked and weird, changing speeds. She's looking at me.

Eddie *(Dialing again and again)*: This really happened to you?

Phil: What can I do, Eddie? Help me.

Eddie: I'm trying.

Phil: So this broad is looking at me. She's givin' me this look. This thing's in my hand, arrrgghhh, like I'm offering to put this goddamn model airplane inside her. It's liable to come apart and throw her across the room.

Eddie: Bonnie, please. *(He slams down the phone.)*

Artie: This thing's goin', arrrggghhh, arrrghhh. Phil's sayin', "Want to come home with me?"

Phil: Arrghhhhh, arghhh, want to come home with me? *(Eddie, on the stool by the phone, stares at Phil.)*

Eddie: You really did this, Phil?

Phil: Yeah.

Eddie: Listen to me. You're a rare human being.

Phil *(Very pleased)*: So how come everything turns to shit?

Eddie: I don't know, but we're going to find out. You're a rare, precious human being.

Phil: I suspected as much.

Eddie: Underneath all this bullshit, you have a real instinctive thing, you know what I mean. It's like this wide open intuition.

Phil (*Rising now, he glides across the room to stand beside Eddie*): This is what I think sometimes about myself.

Eddie: I mean, it's unique; this goddamn imagination—you could channel it.

Phil: I have thoughts sometimes they could break my head open.

Eddie: Whata you mean?

Phil: I mean, these big thoughts. These big goddamn thoughts. I don't know what to do with them.

Eddie: This is what I'm saying: if you could channel them into your talent. I mean, under all this crazed bullshit you've been forced to develop—

Phil: I get desperate. I feel like my thoughts are all just going to burst out of my head and leave me; they're going to pick me up and throw me around the room. I fight with them. It's a bloodbath this monster I have with my thoughts. Maybe if I channeled them.

Eddie: I never took you so seriously before. I mean, quite so seriously.

Phil: Me neither.

Eddie: I'm calling Bonnie, Phil. I'm calling her for you.

Phil: So call her.

Mickey (*Leaning from his window seat toward Artie on the couch*): Could this be it, Artie?

Artie: What? (*Though busy with the phone, Eddie and Phil are clearly eavesdropping on Mickey and Artie.*)

Mickey: Could this be destiny in fact at work, Artie, and we are witnessing it?—the pattern in the randomness, so that we see it: man without a home, careless weights; broken vibrator, disappointed broad. And from this apparent mess, two guys fall in love.

Eddie: He's jealous, Phil. Don't worry about his petty jealousy.

Phil: He could choke on his own spit, I would feel nothing. No. I would feel glee. I would be a kid at an amusement park. *(As Eddie disgustedly hangs up the phone.)* She's still busy?

Eddie: I'm gonna get her for you, Phil, don't worry.

Phil: So who is this bitch she's on the phone forever, some goddamn agent?

Eddie: No, no, she's terrific, you're gonna love her. This is a bitch who dances naked artistically in this club. That's her trip.

Mickey: With a balloon.

Eddie: That's what makes it artistic. Without the balloon, what is she?

Artie: A naked bitch.

Eddie: You would wanna fuck her, though.

Artie: Anybody would.

Eddie: She's a good bitch, though, you know what I mean? She's got a heart of gold.

Mickey: What's artistic about her is her blow jobs.

Phil *(Grabbing Eddie, turning him back to the phone)*: Get her, Eddie; get her.

Mickey: She's critically acclaimed.

Eddie: And the best part about her is that she's up for anything.

Mickey: Like the airport.

Eddie: What airport? *(Then he screams into the phone.)* Bonnie, please!

Mickey: So we ask her to go to the airport.

Eddie (*Remembering, he puts down the phone*): Oh Jesus, the airport!

Eddie moves to Mickey as the story, the claims of old times, the competitiveness of memory and telling the story draw Mickey and Eddie into a teamlike intimacy, leaving Phil to flop down in the big armchair.

Mickey: This was amazing. Robbie Rattigan was coming in.

Eddie: He was coming in, see, he was up for this major part in this pilot for an ABC series. Right? He's flying in, we wanna make him feel welcome.

Mickey: He's gonna be all screwed up from the flight, he's got this big meeting.

Eddie: Bonnie jumps at the chance. She's seen him as a featured killer on several cop shows which he was on almost every one of them as a killer. "Meet him at the airport," we tell her.

Mickey: "He's a friend of ours," we tell her. We want you to relax him on the drive back to town.

Eddie: She says to us that she has been very impressed by his work when she saw it.

Mickey: She's a fuckin' critic.

Eddie: So we meet the plane. Robbie gets off, you know; we meet him, we get in the car. Hey, hey, blah-blah, blah-blah-blah. We're on the freeway, she's in the back seat with Robbie.

Mickey: She's just there.

Eddie: We made a point of just introducing her like she's somebody's girlfriend, you know, or just some bitch we know, she happens to be in the back seat when we pick him up.

Mickey: An accident.

Eddie: No big deal.

Mickey: So Robbie's talkin' about the part he's up for, and getting very serious, "rapateta." So Bonnie reaches over and unzips his fly. He looks at her like she just fell out of a tree. "Don't mind me," she says. *(Having drifted together to the kitchen, Eddie is again on the chair by the phone; Mickey, behind the counter.)*

Eddie: I'm tellin' him to keep on talkin'.

Mickey: We're acting like we don't know what's goin' on.

Eddie: She just had this impulse. He's irresistible.

Mickey: That's the impression.

Eddie: That he's this irresistible guy. That's the impression we want to make.

Mickey: So she's gone down on him.

Eddie: You can tell by his face.

Mickey: She's very energetic.

Eddie *(Dialing one more time)*: So he starts to curse us out. You would not believe the cursing he does.

Mickey: "Robbie," I tell him, "Welcome to L.A.!"

Eddie *(Into the phone)*: Bonnie! Hello! *(Everybody freezes.)* Hello. Hey. Bonnie. Eddie. Yeah. C'mon over. Yeah. C'mon over. *(He hangs up.)* She's comin' over.

Phil: She's comin' over? She's really comin'?

Eddie: Yeah. Oh, the look on Robbie's face, and the look on the kid's face. Remember that?

Mickey: No. What?

Eddie: The kid. Oh, yeah. Christ, the kid. She's got a six-year-old daughter, and she was there.

Mickey: She was with us?

Eddie: In the front seat. I forgot about the kid. Wasn't she there?

Mickey: Yeah. Remember?

Eddie: Yeah.

Mickey: So Robbie's wong comes out, and he's got one. I mean, this guy is epic.

Eddie: Monstrous. The kid is petrified.

Mickey: I mean, there's her mother goin' into combat with this horse.

Eddie: It's a goddamn snake.

Mickey: This is sick, isn't it? I'm gettin' a little sick.

Eddie: We were ripped though, weren't we? We were ripped.

Mickey: Maybe we were blotto.

Eddie: Then we woulda forgot the whole thing. Which we didn't.

Mickey: We nearly did. I mean, about the kid, right?

Eddie: I don't think the mitigating circumstances are sufficient! I ended up takin' care of her. She started to cry, remember?

Mickey: No.

Eddie: Sure. I mean, she didn't start to cry, but she looked like somebody whacked her in the back of the head with a rock. So I hadda take care of her. You remember, Mickey!

Mickey: Almost. I was drivin'. So then what happened? I was personally blotto.

Eddie: Bullshit! We ended up, I'm holdin' her, we're tellin' her these goddamn stories, remember? She was there. We were makin' up this story about elves and shit, and this kingdom full of wild rabbits, and the elves were getting stomped to death by gangs of wild rabbits.

Mickey: Jungle Bunnies, I think, is what we called them.

Eddie: Fuck. Everywhere I turn I gotta face my own depravity. Jungle Bunnies are stomping elves to death so the elves start to hang them. Is that the story?

Mickey: Yeah. And we were doin' the voices. *(Now they are moaning and pounding their heads on the counter in a mix of mock and real remorse.)*

Eddie: I don't wanna think about it. High-pitched, right?

Mickey: Yeah, high-pitched . . .

Mickey and Eddie: And rural!

Eddie: The kid was catatonic. I think maybe that was it, Mickey; we turned the corner in this venture.

Mickey: Right. What venture?

Eddie: Life. That was the nose dive. I mean, where it began. We veered at that moment into utter irredeemable depravity. *(As they collapse upon the counter.)*

Mickey: I feel sick to my stomach about myself. A little. That I could do that. How could I do that?

Phil *(Leaping to his feet)*: Hey! You guys! Don't get crazy! You had a WHIM. This is what happens to people. THEY HAVE WHIMS. So you're sittin' around, Robbie's comin'. You want him to like you, you want him to think well of you. So you have this whim. Did she have to do it? Did anybody twist her arm? *(Mickey and Eddie have straightened slowly.)*

Mickey: Phil's right, Eddie. What'd we do? I mean, objectively. Did anybody say, "Bring your kid."

Eddie: It's the airwaves.

Mickey: Exactly. *(Mickey heads up the stairs.)*

Eddie: TV. TV. Once it was a guy from TV, what chance did she have? *(Phil lounges in the armchair while Artie is flopped on the couch. Mickey goes upstairs and emerges from the bathroom with a huge hashish pipe and a* Variety *with which he flops down on the floor of the balcony.)* She couldn't help herself. And I think subconsciously we knew this. Didn't we know it? I mean, what does she watch? About a million hours of TV a week, so the airwaves are all mixed with the TV waves and then the whole thing is scrambled in her brain waves so, you know, her head is just full of this static, this fog of TV thoughts, to which she refers for everything. I mean, this is an opportunity to mix with the gods we're offering her in the back seat of our car.

As Eddie finishes, he is reclining on top of the kitchen counter, his back against the wall. Mickey has given up reading and is flat on the floor,

his arm dangling through the rails. The door opens and in comes Bon-
nie.

Bonnie: Hi!

Eddie: Bonnie.

Artie: Hi!

Bonnie: Hi, Artie, hi, Mickey. Your call was a miracle, Eddie.

Mickey: Hi.

Eddie: This is Phil.

Bonnie: Hi.

Phil: Hi.

Eddie: He's recently divorced.

Bonnie: Everybody I know is either recently married or recently divorced, some of them the same people. It's a social
epidemic.

Phil: I'm recently divorced.

Bonnie: I've got to have some blow, Eddie, can you spare it?

Eddie: Sure, hey.

Bonnie: Doom and gloom have come to sit in my household
like some permanent kind of domestic appliance. My brain has
been invaded with glop. If you could spare some blow to vac-
uum the lobes, I would be eternally grateful.

Phil: We could go buy some.

Eddie: I got plenty. *(Bonnie has moved to Eddie, who is digging out*
some coke for her as Phil drifts toward them.)

Phil: She and me could go. I know where to buy it like it grows
on trees.

Bonnie: I was in mortal longing for someone to call me. I was
totally without hope of ever having worthwhile companionship
tonight, a decent fucking conversation. *(Phil, sidling up to Bon-*
nie, puts his arm around her as Eddie spoons her some coke.)

Phil: Eddie's got some stuff here to really round off your—you know, rough spots.

Bonnie: I couldn't be happier.

Phil: We been having a good time, too.

Bonnie: Is this particular guy just being ceremonial here with me, Eddie, or does he want to dick me?

Eddie: I thought we'd get around to that later.

Bonnie *(To Phil)*: Eddie thought we'd get around to that later.

Phil *(Hands off, backing away)*: Hey, if I have overstepped some invisible boundary here, you notify me fast because I respond quickly to clear-cut information while, you know, murk and innuendo make me totally demented.

Artie: We couldn't have less of any idea what we're doing here, Bonnie.

Bonnie: I'm sure he has his saving graces.

Mickey: Why don't you list them? I bet he'd like you to list them! *(With this Mickey breaks himself up; Artie erupts in a fit of giggles as Phil tries awkwardly to join in.)*

Phil: You could make a list of what you think might be my saving graces based on some past savings account in the sky.

Bonnie: Is everybody ripped here?

Mickey: We're involved in a wide variety of pharmaceutical experiments. *(This, of course, keeps them laughing.)*

Eddie: Testing the perimeters of the American Dream of oblivion.

Bonnie *(Giving Eddie a little kiss on the forehead)*: Well, I can't express the gratitude for your generosity that led you to including me.

Phil: You want people to call, you might spend less time on the phone.

Bonnie *(Turning to look for Phil, who is sitting on the arm of the couch with a bottle)*: This is exactly my point. This bozo would not get off the phone.

Mickey: You could hang up.

Bonnie *(Moving toward Mickey)*: His reaction was to call me back so quickly I considered whether he had magical powers or not.

Phil: You could leave the phone off the hook.

Bonnie: Which I did. *(As she moves to Phil for the bottle.)*

Phil: This explains the infinite length of your busy signal.

Bonnie *(To Phil)*: See! This is what I was afraid of: Friends might call. You see the dilemma I was in.

Phil *(Almost scolding her)*: Eddie called and called.

Eddie: We called as if it was a religious duty.

Bonnie: Thank god you persisted. *(She crosses to Eddie.)* This guy was pushing me beyond my own rational limits so I was into hallucinatory kinds of, you know, considerations, like would I invite him over and then hack him to death with a cleaver.

Phil: Who is this guy? *(Moving after her, he drops into the armchair, kneeling in the seat looking over the back toward her and Eddie.)* I know ways to make guys stop anything. They might think they couldn't live without it until I talk to them. They might think they have the courage of cowboys, but I can change their minds. Who is this guy?

Bonnie: This is what I'm getting at, Eddie, a person like this guy can only be found in your household. What's your name again?

Phil: Phil.

Artie: He's dangerous, Bonnie.

Bonnie: Who isn't?

Artie: I mean, in ways you can't imagine.

Bonnie: That's very unlikely, Artie. *(Eddie hands her a lighted joint.)* Drugs. I mean, I'm telling this guy on the phone that drugs are and just have been as far as I can remember, an ever-present component of my personality. I am a drug-person.

And I would not, if I were him, consider that anything un-usual, unless he is compelled to reveal to the entire world his ignorance of the current situation in which most people find themselves—so that's what I'm telling this guy.

Phil: Who is this guy? He's drivin' me nuts, this guy.

Bonnie: Some guy. Don't worry about it. (*Crossing to Phil to give him a joint and almost to console him with her explanation, as she sits on the hassock beside the armchair.*) I mean, my life in certain of its segments has just moved into some form of automation on which it runs as if my input is no longer required. So my girl-friend Sarah gets involved with this guy who is totally freaked out on EST, so she gets proportionally freaked out on EST, this is what love can do to you, so then they are both attempting to freak me out on EST, as if my certainty that they are utterly full of shit is some non-negotiable threat to them rather than just my opinion and so they must—out of their insecurity, as-sault me with this goddamn EST ATTACK so that everywhere I turn I am confronted with their booklets and god knows what else, these pictures of this Werner Shmerner and the key to them that I must get rid of is my drug-desires, which is the subject of their unending, unvaried, you know, whatchamacal-lit.

Eddie: Proselytizing.

Bonnie (*Looking to Eddie*): They will not shut up about it. So I am trying to make to this guy what is for me an obvious point, which is that unlike those who have lost their minds to EST, I am a normal person: I need my drugs! (*Phil has coke which he gives her. They have booze to share, grass.*) Has he been in the hos-pital lately? I am asking him. Because you go in the hospital, where I have recently had reason to go, and along with every-thing else you can get there, the anesthesiologist, the minute I am strong enough, he is offering to sell me coke of which he says he is himself deeply fond along with twenty or thirty per-cent of the nurses and a sprinkling of the interns, as he re-ported it. I am scoffed at for this remark, so, being civilized, I attempt to support my point with what Sarah and I both know from our mutual girlfriend Denise. "Does Denise not work as a legal secretary in this building full of lawyers?" I tell him.

Well, she says these lawyers are totally blow oriented, and you go in there in the after-hours where some of them are still working, it sounds like a goddamn hog farm, she says. Well, Sarah and this guy react to this with two absolutely unaltered onslaughts, and while they're yelling at me, I'm yelling at them, that since I am a drug person, I must give them a drug person's answer: *(Sliding off the hassock to the pillows on the floor.)* "Thbgggggggggghhhhhhhggggggghhhhh!" I go, and slam down the phone and hang it up. *(Ending up lying on her back on the floor at Phil's feet.)*

Phil: So that's when we called.

Bonnie: When I picked it up, you were there. Eddie was there.

Phil: And now you're here.

Mickey *(Gazing down on Phil and Bonnie)*: Is this the hand of destiny again, Eddie, look at it.

Eddie *(Still lying on the counter)*: I'm looking.

Mickey: The hand of destiny again emerging just enough from, you know, all the normal muck and shit, so that, you know, we get a glimpse of it.

Bonnie: Whata you mean, Mickey? What's he mean?

Eddie: It's a blind date.

Bonnie: Ohh, you invited me over for this guy, Eddie?

Eddie: Yeah. Why?

Bonnie: Oh, you know, I thought. . . .

Phil: She don't have to, Eddie. *(Phil storms away toward the kitchen.)*

Bonnie: No, no, I just didn't know it was a setup.

Phil *(Behind the counter getting a beer)*: I mean, she should know it could be the final straw for me to justify some sort of butchery, but that's just a fact of life and not in any way meant to influence the thing here.

Eddie *(Dropping off the counter, Eddie moves to join Bonnie on the floor)*: You disappointed in Phil?

Bonnie: I wasn't thinking about it.

Eddie: What were you thinking about?

Bonnie: Eddie, look, it doesn't matter.

Eddie: He's nervous.

Phil *(At the counter with his drink)*: I'm very nervous.

Bonnie *(Standing up)*: Right. So what's the agenda?

Eddie *(Giving her some coke)*: Hey, I figured I'd just sort of rough in the outline, you'd have the rest at your fingertips; you know, operating at an instinctual level.

Bonnie *(Walking to Phil, she spoons coke to his nose, and he snorts)*: So you wanna go upstairs? *(Phil shakes his head no.)* No?

Phil: Out. Eddie, can I borrow your car? I don't have a car.

Bonnie: So we'll go over to my place. *(Picking up a joint.)* Can I take this, Eddie?

Eddie: What happened to your car?

Phil: My wife got all the keys. She put one a those locks on it so it fuckin' screams at you.

Bonnie: I got a car.

Phil: You got a car? *(Bonnie is running around, collecting supplies, picking up her shoes.)*

Bonnie: So we'll be back in a little, you guys'll be here?

Eddie: Where else?

Bonnie: Bye.

Mickey *(As Bonnie and Phil go out the door)*: Have a nice time, kids.

Eddie: Bye.

Mickey: She's some bitch.

Eddie *(Settling back on the pillows on the floor)*: Balloons. Balloons.

Artie (*Lounging, staring at the ceiling*): Eddie, can I ask you something? I wanna ask you something.

Eddie: Sure.

Artie: You don't mind?

Eddie: What?

Artie: I'm just very curious about the nature of certain patterns of bullshit by which people pull the wool over their own eyes.

Eddie: Yeah?

Artie: So could you give me a hint as to the precise nature of the delusion with which you hype yourself about this guy, that you treat him the way you do?

Eddie: Artie, hey, you know, I have a kind of intuitive thing with Phil. Don't get in a fuckin' snit about it.

Artie: Because you desert me for this fucking guy all the time. What is it about you, you gotta desert me?

Eddie: I don't desert you.

Artie (*Rising now, he moves toward Eddie*): But what is it you really think about me, so that in your estimation you can dump on me, and treat Phil like he's some—I don't know what—but you lost a paternity suit and he was the result.

Eddie: Artie, you're the only one old enough around here to be everybody's father, so what are you talking about?

Artie: Age don't mean shit in a situation like this.

Eddie: First of all, I don't consider your statement that I dump on you accurate, so why should I defend against it? (*Slowly now, Eddie is getting to his feet, his back to Artie.*)

Artie: It's subtle. Hey, you think that means I'm gonna miss it? It's an ongoing, totally pervasive attitude with which you dump on me subtly so that it colors almost every remark, every gesture. And I'm sick of it.

Eddie (*Turning, he faces Artie*): I'm sorry your deal fell through. (*And walks away, looking for something, heading toward Mickey, who*

lies on the balcony as he has been, arm dangling, watching every-
thing.)

Artie: You lie to yourself, Eddie.

Eddie: Yeah?

Artie *(Pursuing Eddie)*: That's right. You lie to yourself.

Eddie *(As Mickey hands Eddie the big hashish pipe)*: Just because
you're Jewish doesn't make you Freud, you prick.

Artie: And just because you're whatever the fuck you are
doesn't make you whatever the hell you think you are. The
goddamn embodiment of apple pie here is full of shit.

Eddie *(Sitting down on the stairs to light the pipe)*: So I lie, huh?
Who better? I'm a very good liar, and I'm very gullible. This
makes for an accomplishment in the field never before imagined.

Artie: And my deal didn't fall through, anyway. That's just
stunningly diversionary on your part even if it did. Which it
didn't. You're a deceptive sonofabitch, Eddie. Is everything a
ploy to you?

Eddie: What are you talking about?

Artie: You know what I mean.

Eddie: I don't.

Artie: The hell you don't. Doesn't he Mickey? He knows.

Eddie: I don't. I swear it.

Artie: You're just avoiding the goddamn confrontation here.

Eddie: What confrontation?

Artie: We're having a confrontation here.

Eddie: We are?

Artie: Yeah! I am! I'm gettin' out of here. Mickey, you wanna
get out of here?

Mickey: Sure. *(Artie starts up the stairs, but Eddie blocks the way.)*

Eddie: Where you goin'?

Artie: I'm goin' to the can, and then I'm getting out of here. *(He squeezes past Eddie.)* And you, you sonofabitch, I'm going to tell you the goddamn bottom line because if you don't know it, you are—I mean, a thousandfold—just utterly—and you fucking know it!

Eddie: What?

Artie *(Retreating toward the door of the bathroom)*: Hey, you don't have to deal any further with my attempts at breathing life into this corpse of our friendship. Forget about it. *(He bolts into the bathroom, slamming the door.)*

Eddie: You're a schmuck, Artie! You're a schmendrick! Go check your messages! *(Flopping down on the stairs, he turns to Mickey, lying on the balcony floor just above Eddie's head.)* What was that?

Mickey *(Unmoving)*: I think what he was trying to get at is that he, you know, considers your investment in Phil, which is in his mind sort of disproportionate and maybe even—and mind you, this is Artie's thought, not mine—but maybe even fraudulent and secretly self-serving on your part. So you know, blah-blah-blah, rapateta—that this investment is based on the fact that Phil is very safe because no matter how far you manage to fall, Phil will be lower. You end up crawling along the sidewalk, Phil's gonna be on his belly in the gutter looking up in wide-eyed admiration. *(Bolting upright, Eddie heads for the couch, where he grabs up a bottle.)*

Eddie: This is what Artie thinks.

Mickey *(Getting slowly to his feet now, Mickey starts dressing to go out with Artie: putting on a belt, tucking in a shirt, putting on his shoes)*: Yeah. And it hurts his feelings, because, you know, he'd like to think he might be capable of an eyeball-to-eyeball relationship with you based not necessarily on equality, but on, nevertheless, some real affinity—and if not the actuality, at least the possibility of respect. So your, you know, decision, or whatever—compulsion—to shortchange yourself, in his estimation, and hang out with Phil is for him a genuine disappointment, which you just saw the manifestation of.

Eddie *(Has been drinking quite a bit throughout the evening and is now taking in great quantities, throwing his head back to drink from the bottle)*: That was his hurt feelings.

Mickey: Yeah.

Eddie: What's everybody on my case for all of a sudden?

Mickey: Nobody's on your case.

Eddie: What do you think you're doing, then, huh? What is this? What was Artie doing?

Mickey *(Having descended the stairs, Mickey is now sitting down in the armchair, putting on his shoes)*: You have maybe some misconceptions is all, first of all about how smart you are. And then maybe even if you are as smart as you think you are, you have some misconception about what that entitles you to regarding your behavior to other human beings. Such facts being pointed out is what's going on here, that's all. Don't take it personally.

Eddie: What would make you mad, Mickey?

Mickey: Hey, I'm sure it's possible. *(Mickey moves now into the kitchen, looking for something to eat in the refrigerator.)*

Eddie: What would it be? I'm trying to imagine.

Mickey: The truth is, Artie isn't really that pissed at you anyway.

Eddie: He got close enough.

Mickey: You know, his feelings got hurt.

Eddie: That's what I'm talking about. Don't I have feelings, too?

Mickey *(Standing at the breakfast nook, eating ice cream)*: Except it makes him feel good to have his feelings hurt, that's why he likes you. You're a practicing prick. You berate him with the concoction of moral superiority which no doubt reassures him everything is as it should be, sort of reminding him in a cozy way of his family in whose eyes he basked most of his life as a glowing disappointment.

Eddie: You're just too laid back for human tolerance some-times, Mickey. A person wonders if you really care.

Mickey: I get excited.

Eddie: You have it figured somehow. What's it according to—some schematic arrangement—grids of sophistication—what's the arrangement by which you assess what's what so you are left utterly off the hook?

Mickey: It's a totally unconscious process.

Eddie: Fuck you, Mickey.

Mickey: Ask Darlene if she won't let you go back to coke, why don't you? Booze seems to bring out some foul-spirited streak in you.

Eddie: That's the fucking bottom line, though, huh, nobody's going to take substantial losses in order to align and endure with what are totally peripheral—I mean, transient elements in their life. I mean, we all know we don't mean shit in one another's eyes, finally.

Mickey: Do you realize you're turning nasty right before my eyes?

Eddie: I'm feeling a little grim, if you don't mind. *(He takes a drink.)*

Mickey: Just so you're aware of it.

Eddie: Hey, if I wasn't, there's plenty of judgmental jerks around here to remind me. *(He takes another drink.)*

Mickey: You gonna remember any of this tomorrow, or is this one of your, you know, biodegradable moments?

Eddie: Lemme in on your point of view, Mickey, we can have a dialectic.

Mickey: Hey. Just in case you notice me walk out of the room, you can reflect back on this, all right?

Eddie: All right. On what?

Mickey *(Now backing toward the door)*: That, you know, this foul mood of yours might have been sufficient provocation to motivate my departure, see. You know, lock that in so you can minimize the paranoia.

Eddie: You sound like my goddamn mother.

Artie (*As coming out of the bathroom, he starts down the stairs*): Father.

Eddie: Mother.

Artie: So you coming with us, Eddie, or not?

Eddie (*Slumped on the couch, drinking*): Where you going?

Artie: I don't know. Where we going, Mickey?

Mickey: It was your idea.

Eddie: No.

Mickey (*To Eddie*): We'll go somewhere. We'll think of somewhere; change the mood.

Eddie: No. Fuck no. I'm gonna get ripped and rant at the tube.

Mickey: What's a matter with you?

Eddie: Nothing.

Artie: You don't wanna.

Eddie: No. (*As Mickey, shrugging, goes strolling out the door.*)

Artie: You gonna be all right?

Eddie: Who cares?

Artie: This is not caring I'm expressing here. This is curiosity. Don't misconstrue the behavior here and confuse yourself that anybody cares!

Mickey (*From off*): Artie, let's go.

Eddie: Artie, relax. You're starting to sound like an imitation of yourself, and you're hardly tolerable the first time.

Artie: Eddie, don't worry about a thing. This is just some sort of irreversible chemical pollution of your soul. Your body has just gone into shock from all the shit you've taken in, so you're suffering some form of virulent terminal toxic nastiness. Nothing to worry about.

Artie, with his last word, is out the door, and the phone is ringing. Eddie looks at the phone and starts toward it.

Eddie: Who's worried? The only thing worrying me, Artie, was that you might decide to stay. *(Grabbing up the phone.)* Yeah. Agnes. Whata you want? *(As he talks, he arranges a nest of pillows onto which he flops with the phone and his bottle of vodka.)* I said, were you worried I might be having a pleasant evening, you didn't want to take any chances that I might not be miserable enough without hearing from you? No, I did not make an obscene call to you. What'd he say? It can't be too dirty to say, Agnes, HE said it. Every call you make to me is obscene. Everything you say to me is obscene. Of course I'm drunk. If you don't want to talk to me when I'm drunk, call me in the daytime. I'm sober in the daytime, but of course we both know you do want to talk to me when I'm drunk. You get off on it, don't you. Reminds you of the good old days. If you hurt my little girl, I'll kill you . . . I said, "If you hurt my little girl, I'll kill you!"

Bonnie enters through the front door, her clothing ripped and dirty, her knee scraped. Limping, she carries one of her shoes in her hand. Seeing her, Eddie gets to his feet.

Bonnie: Eddie . . . !

Eddie *(Into the phone)*: I have to go. I'll call you tomorrow. Goodbye. *(He hurries toward Bonnie who, leaning against one of the balcony support beams, starts hobbling toward him.)* Where's Phil?

Bonnie: You know, Eddie, how come you gotta put me at the mercy of such a creep for? Can I ask you that?

Eddie: Where is he? *(He is helping her toward the armchair.)*

Bonnie: He threw me out of my own car, Eddie.

Eddie: What'd you do?

Bonnie *(Pulling away from him, slapping at his arms in a little fit)*: Whata you mean, what'd I do? He's a fucking guy, he should be in a ward somewhere! You could have at least warned me!

Eddie *(Struggling to help her)*: Nobody listens to me.

Bonnie *(Still pushing or hitting at him)*: I listen to you and you damn well know it.

Eddie: You're all right. *(Patting her, as she sits in the armchair, he heads for the bar to make her a drink and wet a washcloth in the sink with which to wash off her knee.)*

Bonnie: I'm alive, if that's what you mean, but I am haunted by the suspicion that it is strictly a matter of luck. Nor is it enough that I have my various limbs, you know, operational. I wouldn't mind having a little, you know—LIKE A GOD-DAMN, YOU KNOW, A SLEEPING CAT HAS IT!

Eddie: Contentment.

Bonnie: I'm a nervous wreck! This guy is a debilitating experience. I mean, you should reconsider your entire evaluation of this guy, Eddie. *(Hobbling toward him, as if with urgent news.)* This is a guy, he is totally without redeeming social value!

Eddie *(Handing her the drink, he guides her back to the chair)*: Where is he?

Bonnie: I mean, I came down here in good faith, Eddie, I hope you are not going to miss that point.

Eddie *(As he kneels down to tend her knee with the washcloth)*: Will you get off your high horse about Phil, all right? So he took your car, so what. He'll bring it back.

Bonnie: He didn't just take my car, Eddie; HE THREW ME OUT OF IT.

Eddie *(Trying to shrug the whole thing off)*: So what?

Bonnie *(Ripping the washcloth from his hands)*: Whata you mean, "so what?"

Eddie: So what? *(Reaching to get the washcloth back.)*

Bonnie: Eddie, it was moving!

Eddie: He slowed it down. *(Still he tries to get the washcloth, but she will not let him have it.)*

Bonnie: Right. He slowed it down. But he didn't slow it down enough. I mean, he didn't stop the fucking car. He slowed it down. Whata you mean, "he slowed it down?" As if that was enough to make a person feel, you know, appropriately handled. He threw me out of my own slowly moving car and nearly killed me.

Eddie (*Indicating her knee which is right in front of him*): You scraped your knee!

Bonnie: I just missed cracking open my head on a boulder that was beside the road.

Eddie: What boulder?

Bonnie: Whata you mean, what boulder? This boulder beside the road. THAT boulder.

Eddie: Will you please get to the fucking point?

Bonnie: No.

Eddie: Then shut up! (*Whirling, he flops furiously back on his pillows. Grabbing up his bottle, he drinks.*)

Bonnie: No! (*Rising now, she starts to angrily pull off her skirt and then her pantyhose in order to tend to her knee and other wounds.*) Because what I wanna know about maybe is you, and why you would put a friend of yours like me in that kind of jeopardy. Why you would let me go with this creep, if I was begging, let alone instigate it, that's what I'm wondering when I get right down to it, though I hadn't even thought about it. But maybe it's having a goddamn friendship with you is the source of jeopardy for a person. (*Swinging her skirt at him, she storms over to the bar for more to drink, for water and ice for her wounds.*)

Eddie (*His feelings have been hurt: as far as he's concerned, he's been trying to help*): You want to take that position.

Bonnie: It could be.

Eddie: You wanna—you take it if you want to.

Bonnie: I'm not sayin' I want to. I'm saying maybe I should want to, and if I think about it, maybe that's what I'll do and you ought to know I am going to think about it.

Due to his drinking, Eddie, from the instant Bonnie first hurled the shoe or hit at him, has been reacting increasingly as a little boy. Scolded by Artie and scolded by Mickey, he tries to hold his ground against Bonnie, yet to placate her. When she yells at him, he winces, as if her words are physical. Behind her back he sometimes mimics her as she talks. When she, out of her own frustration, swings at him with a shoe, a blouse, her pantyhose, he recoils as a child might. Though he is attempting to contend with Bonnie, he is far away and with someone from long ago.

Eddie: Don't, you know, strain yourself.

Bonnie: I hurt my foot, too, and my hip and my elbow along with my knee.

Eddie: I'm sorry about that.

Bonnie: Maybe you might show something more along the lines of your feelings and how you might explain yourself so that I might have them to think about when I'm thinking about it all, so I give you a fair shot. I mean, this guy, Eddie, is not just, you know, semi-weird; he is working on genuine berserk. Haven't you noticed some clue to this?

Eddie: You must have done SOMETHING.

Bonnie: I SAT THERE. *(Behind the bar, she drinks, puts ice on her wounds.)* He drove; I listened to the music on the tape deck like he wanted, and I tol' him the sky was pretty, just trying, you know, to put some sort of fucking humanity into the night, some sort of spirit so we might, you know, appear to one another as having had at one time or another a thought in our heads and were not just these totally fuck-oriented, you know, things with clothes on.

Eddie: What are you getting at?

Bonnie: What I'm getting at is I did nothing, and in addition, I am normally a person who allots a certain degree of my energy to being on the alert for creeps, Eddie. I am not so dumb as to be ignorant of the vast hordes of creeps running loose in California as if every creep with half his screws loose has slid here like the continent is tilted. But because this guy was on your recommendation, I am caught unawares and nearly maimed. That's what I'm getting at. I mean, this guy is driving, so I tell him we can go to my house. He says he's hungry, so I say, "Great, how about a Jack-In-The-Box?" He asks me if that's code for something. So I tell him, "No, it's California-talk, we have a million of 'em, is he new in town?" His answer is, do I have a water bed? "No," I tell him, but we could go to a sex motel, they got water beds. They got porn on the in-house video. Be great! So then I detect he's lookin' at me, so I smile, and he says, "Whata you smilin' about?" I say, "Whata you mean?" He says, like he's talkin' to the steering wheel, "Whata you thinkin'?" or some shit. I mean, but it's like to the steering wheel; he's all bent out of shape.

Eddie: See. You did something.

Bonnie: What?

Eddie: I don't know.

Bonnie: I smiled.

Eddie: Then what?

Bonnie (*Hitting at him with her pantyhose*): I smiled, Eddie, for chrissake, I smiled is what I did. It's a friendly thing in most instances, but for him it promotes all this paranoid shit he claims he can read in it my secret opinions of him, which he is now saying. The worst things anybody could think about anybody, but I ain't saying nothing. He's sayin' it. Then he screams he knew this venture was a one-man operation and the next thing I know he's trying to push me out of the car. He's trying to drive it, and slow it down, and push me out all at once, so we're swervin' all over the road. So that's what happened. You get it now?

Eddie: He's been having a rough time.

Bonnie: Eddie, it's a rough century all the way around—you say so yourself, Eddie. Who does anybody know who is doing okay? So this is some sort of justification for us all to start pushing each other out of cars?—things aren't working out personally the way we planned?

Eddie: Aren't you paying any fucking attention to my point here? I'm talking about a form of desperation you are maybe not familiar with it.

Bonnie: Oh.

Eddie: I'm talking about a man here, a guy he's had his entire thing collapse. Phil has been driven to the brink.

Bonnie: Oh. Okay. *(Now, angrily, Bonnie begins to dress.)* You consider desperation you and your friend's own, private, so-called—thingamajig. Who would have thought other? I mean, I can even understand that due to the attitude I know you hold me in, which is of course mainly down. Because deep down, a person does not live in an aura of—you know, which we all have them, auras—and they spray right out of us and they are just as depressing and pushy on the people in our company as anything we might, you know, knowingly and overtly bad-mouth them with. But at the same time, you certainly should be told that in my opinion you are totally, one hundred per-cent, you know, with your head up your ass about me.

Eddie: Yeah.

Bonnie: That's what I'm saying. "Wrong," is what I'm saying. See, because I am a form of human being just like any other, get it! And you wanna try holding onto things on the basis of your fingernails, give me a call. So desperation, believe it or not, is within my areas of expertise, you understand? I am a person whose entire life with a child to support depends on her tits and this balloon and the capabilities of her physical grace and imaginary inventiveness with which I can appear to express something of interest in the air by my movement and places in the air I put the balloon along with my body, which some other dumb bitch would be unable to imagine or would fall down in the process of attempting to perform in front of crowds of totally incomprehensible and terrifying bunch of au-dience members. And without my work what am I but an un-employed scrunt on the meat market of these streets? Because this town is nothin' but mean in spite of the palm trees. So that's my point about desperation, and I can give you refer-ences, just in case you never thought of it, you know; and just thought I was over here—some mindless twat over here with blonde hair and big eyes.

Eddie: I hadn't noticed your hair or eyes.

Bonnie: I'm gonna level with you, Eddie, I came here for a ride home and an apology. *(Finished dressing, she pivots furiously and starts for the door.)*

Eddie *(Rising up on his knees)*: Don't you fuck everybody you meet?

Bonnie: Whata you mean? WHAT?

Eddie: You know what I'm talking about.

Bonnie *(Coming back at him)*: I fuck who I want. What does one thing have to do with—I mean, what's the correlation, huh?

Eddie *(He is headed toward her on his knees)*: You fuck everybody.

Bonnie: I fuck a lot of different guys: That's just what I do. It's interesting. You know that. You learn a lot about 'em. That's no reason to assume I can be thrown out of a car as random recreation, however. If I want to jump, I'll jump. Not that that's the point, I hope.

Eddie: It's not far from it.

Bonnie: I mean, I fuck different guys so I know the difference. That's what I'm saying. There's a lot of little subtleties go right by you don't have nothing to compare them to.

Eddie: But you're getting these airs is what I'm getting at. I mean you're assuming some sort of posture, like some attitude of I pushed you into some terrible, unfamiliar circumstances and normally you're very discreet about who you ball and who you don't, when normally you—

Bonnie: He coulda hurt me, Eddie.

Eddie *(Trying to stand up)*: I don't care!

Bonnie: Don't tell me that.

Eddie *(Eddie careens backward against the stairway and bounces forward onto the floor on his hands and knees)*: You're just some bitch who thinks it matters that you run around with balloons and your tits out. Nobody's going to take substantial losses over what are totally peripheral, totally transient elements. You know, we're all just background in one another's life. Card-

board cutouts bumping around in this vague, you know, hurlyburly, this spin-off of what was once prime time life; so don't
hassle me about this interpersonal fuck-up on the highway,
okay? *(Having struggled to the sink, he is putting water on his face.)*

Bonnie: You oughta have some pity.

Eddie: I'm savin' it.

Bonnie: For your buddies.

Eddie: For myself. *(The front door opens and Phil bursts in, sweat-
ing, looking worried, clutching a handkerchief.)*

Bonnie: Oh, no. *(Bonnie flees away from Phil toward Eddie behind
the counter.)*

Phil: I'm perfectly, you know, back to earth now. I can understand if you don't believe me, but there's nothing to be concerned about.

Bonnie: I oughta call the cops, you prick.

Phil: You car's just outside; it's okay.

Bonnie: I'm talking about murder almost.

Phil *(Grabbing the phone as if he will present it to her)*: You want
me to dial it for you, Bonnie; you have every right.

Eddie: Shut up. Can you do that? Can you just SHUT UP?
(Grabbing the phone from Phil, he storms away from both of them.)

Phil: I'm sorry, Eddie.

Eddie: I mean, I'm disgusted with the both of you.

Phil: I don't blame you, Eddie.

Eddie *(Trying to get away, to be alone, he goes to the far corner, the
couch. Done with them, he grabs up a newspaper, yet he is too angry)*:
I did my best for the both of you. I did everything I could to
set you up nicely, but you gotta fuck it up. Why is that?

Phil: I'm some kind of very, very unusual jerk, is what I figure.

Bonnie: You had no rhyme nor reason for what you did to me.

HURLYBURLY

Phil (*Following after Eddie, perhaps sitting down next to Eddie, as in an odd way he's giving an explanation for Eddie's sake*): It's broads, Eddie. I got all this hubbub for a personality with which I try to make do, but they see right through it to where I am invisible. I see 'em see through; it makes me crazy, but it ain't their fault.

Eddie: I go out of my way for you, Phil; I don't know what more I can do. Now I have Artie pissed at me, I have Bonnie pissed.

Phil: She has every right; you have every right. Artie's pissed, too?

Eddie: You know that.

Phil: I didn't know it.

Eddie: In your heart I'm talkin' about, Phil; that's what I'm talking about.

Phil: It's—you know, my imaginary side, Eddie—like we were sayin', I get lost in it. I gotta channel it into my work more.

Eddie: Fuck your work. What work? (*Getting up, backing away, yet towering over Phil.*) You don't have any work, Phil, you're background, don't you know that? They just take you on for background. They got all these bullshit stories they want to fill the air with, they want to give them some sense of reality, some fucking air of authenticity, don't they? So they take some guy like you and stick him around the set to make the whole load of shit look real. Don't you know that? You're a prop. The more guys like you they got looking like the truth, the more bullshit they can spread all around you. You're like a tree, Phil. (*Phil is standing.*) You're like the location! They just use you to make the bullshit look legitimate! (*Grabbing up a vodka bottle from the coffee table.*)

Phil: What about my, you know, talent; you said I ought to . . . you know. . . . Remember?

Eddie (*Moving to slump down in the rocking chair*): That was hype. I don't know what I was doin'.

Phil: Oh.

Eddie: Hype. You know.

Phil: You were what—puttin' me on?

Eddie: This is the real goods.

Phil: You mean, all that you said about how I oughta, you know, have some faith in myself, it wasn't true.

Eddie: Whata you think? Did you ever really believe it?

Phil: Yeah. Sorta.

Eddie: Not really. No.

Phil: Well, you know. No.

Eddie: So who we been kiddin'?

Phil: Me. We been kiddin' me. *(Moving nearer to Eddie now.)* But this is the real goods . . . now, right? I mean, we're gettin' down to the real goods now.

Eddie: Yeah.

Phil: So you musta decided it would be best for me to hear the truth.

Eddie: Naw.

Phil: So I could try and straighten myself out. *(By this eerie, unrelenting positiveness, Phil seems to be almost demanding an escalation from Eddie.)*

Eddie: I'm just sick of you, Phil.

Phil: Oh. How long you been sick of me? It's probably recent.

Eddie: No.

Phil: So it's been a long time. . . . So what caused it?

Eddie: I'm gonna let you off the hook now, Phil. I'm not gonna say any more. *(Clutching his newspaper and bottle, Eddie bolts away, heading for the stairs.)*

Phil: You gotta.

Eddie: I'm gonna lighten up. I'm gonna give you a break.

Phil (*Grabbing Eddie partway up the stairs*): Eddie, you gotta give me the entire thing now. I don't need a break. I want it all. I can take it. It's for my own good, right? I can take it. I gotta have it. I got a tendency to kid myself everything is okay. So, you know, you tell me what are the things about me that are for you, you know, disgusting. I want to know. Tell me what they are.

Eddie: Everything. Everything about you.

Phil: Everything? Everything? You really had me fooled, Eddie.

Eddie: That was the point. (*Nodding, he slumps head bowed, on the stairs.*)

Bonnie: You guys are crazy.

Eddie: Whata you mean? (*Looking drunkenly up at Phil.*) What does she mean? You . . . look terrible, Phil. (*As trying to stand, he slips and bumps down several steps.*)

Bonnie: You ain't lookin' so good yourself, Eddie.

Eddie: I feel awful.

Bonnie: Whatsamatter?

Eddie: I dunno. I'm depressed.

Phil: What about?

Eddie: Everything. (*Gesturing, the newspaper still in his hand, he notices it.*) You read this shit. Look at this shit.

Phil: You depressed about the news, Eddie?

Eddie: Yeh.

Phil: You depressed about the newspaper?

Eddie: It's depressing. You read about this fucking neutron bomb? Look at this. (*Hands a part of the paper to Phil, as Bonnie is inching nearer. Phil sits on the arm of the couch, looking at the paper. Eddie, clutching a part of the paper, is trying to stand.*)

Phil: It's depressing. You depressed about the neutron bomb, Eddie?

Eddie: Yeah.

There is an element here of hope in both Bonnie and Phil that Eddie may tell them something to explain, in fact, what's been going on.

Bonnie: It's depressing. *(Kneeling on the armchair, she looks over the back at Eddie and Phil with their newspapers.)* The newspaper is very depressing. I get depressed every time I read it.

Eddie: I mean, not that I would suggest that, you know, the anxiety of this age is an unprecedented anxiety, but I'm fucking worried about it, you know. *(Taking a big drink, which empties the bottle he has.)*

Phil: So it's the newspaper and all the news got you down, huh, Eddie?

Eddie *(Crossing with his tattered newspaper to the coffee table for another bottle sitting there)*: I mean, the aborigine had a lot of problems—nobody is going to say he didn't—tigers in the trees, dogs after his food; and in the Middle Ages, there was goblins and witches in the woods. But this neutron bomb has come along and this sonofabitch has got this ATTITUDE. I mean, inherent in the conception of it is this fucking ATTITUDE about what is worthwhile in the world and what is worth preserving. And do you know what this fastidious prick has at the top of its hierarchy—what sits at the pinnacle? THINGS! *(He takes a huge drink of vodka.)* Put one down in the vicinity of this room and we're out. The three of us—out, out, out! "Well, I think I'll go downtown tomorrow and buy some new shoe—" WHACK! You're out! *(He goes reeling toward the kitchen.)* "Well, I thought I'd apologize for my reprehensible—" You're out! No shoes, no apologize. But guess what? The glasses don't even crack. *(He has a glass.)* The magazine's fine. The chairs, the table—*(He knocks a chair over.)* The phone'll ring if there's anybody to call. The things are unfucking-disturbed. It annihilates people and saves THINGS. It loves things. It is a thing that loves things. Technology has found a way to save its own ass! And whether we know it or not, we KNOW it—that's eating at us. *(Lurching now, he grabs up a wastebasket, appears about to vomit in it, clutches it.)* And where other, older, earlier people—the Ancients might have had some consolation from a view of the heavens as inhabited by this thoughtful, you know, meditative, maybe a trifle unpredictable and wrathful, but nevertheless UP THERE—this divine on-looker—(*Staggering about with his bottle and basket.*)—we have bureaucrats devoted to the accumulation of incomprehensible data—we have connoisseurs of graft and the filibuster—vir-tuosos of the three-martini lunch for whom we vote on the basis of their personal appearance. The air's bad, the water's got poison in it, and into whose eyes do we find ourselves star-ing when we look for providence? We have emptied out the heavens and put oblivion in the hands of a bunch of aging insurance salesmen whose jobs are insecure. (*He ends up leaning against the counter, the basket under his arm, the bottle in his hand.*)

Bonnie: Yeah, well, Eddie, it's no reason to be mean to your friends.

Eddie: Says you.

Bonnie: Exactly.

Eddie: You want me to have reasons? I got to have fucking reasons? (*Suddenly woozy, Eddie is trying to move away, collapsing onto his hands and knees and crawling.*) And you probably want me to say them, don't you. And you probably want them to be the right reasons, and I say them. They're whores, don't you know that? Logic is a slut. Be consoled that inasmuch as you are indiscreet you are logical.

Phil (*Jumping to his feet, heading for the door*): I gotta get some-thing from the car.

Eddie: What?

Phil: I'll be right back. (*He goes out the door.*)

Eddie: No. I say no. You want me "nice." You want me "polite." "Good." (*Crawling as he talks, dragging along his bottle and basket.*) "Kinder." "More considerate." But I say no. I will be a thing. I will be a thing and loved; a thing and live. (*At his nest of pillows, he drops.*) Be harder, colder, a rock or polyurethane, that's my advice. Be a thing and live . . . that's my advice. . . . (*He is on his back now, clutching his garbage can and his bottle. He turns onto his side as if to sleep. Bonnie walks to him and stands looking down.*)

Bonnie: Boy, Eddie, you are just transforming right before my eyes, and I used to have an entirely optimistic opinion of you. What is going on with you? *(She pokes him with her foot.)*

Eddie *(He tries to look up)*: Pardon me?

Bonnie: You know what I'm saying. I mean, you were once upon a time a totally admirable person, but it's reached the point I feel like a goddamn magnifying glass couldn't find what's left of your good points.

Eddie: Suck my dick.

Bonnie: I'm being serious here, Eddie, I thought you had this girlfriend and it was a significant, you know, mutually fulfilling relationship, but you're hardly a viable social entity at the moment, that's what I think.

Eddie: Things have taken a turn for the worse, that's all. Suck my dick, Bonnie.

Bonnie: Like what?

Eddie: Everything has gotten relatively unconventional within me, but who'm I going to complain to? *(Turning away as if to hide or sleep.)* Who's listenin'? And even if they are, what can they do about it?

Bonnie: I'm listenin'.

Eddie: She doesn't love me.

Bonnie: Who?

Eddie: My girlfriend.

Bonnie: Whata you mean?

Eddie: Whata you mean, whata I mean? She doesn't love me. *(Trying to get away, crawling, and dragging with him his bottle, his garbage can, his pillow. He doesn't get far, but has a new nest of sorts.)* Is that some sort of arcane, totally off-the-wall, otherworldly sentiment that I am some oddity to find distressing so that nobody to whom I mention it has any personal reference by which they can understand me? What is going on here? My girlfriend doesn't love me.

Bonnie: Sure she does.

Eddie: No.

Bonnie: Why?

Eddie: I don't know, but she doesn't.

Bonnie: Are you sure?

Eddie *(Angry, pounding on the pillow in petulance, having a little fit)*: She's out of town all the time. She's always out of town. She takes every job that comes across her desk, you know, as long as it takes her out of town.

Bonnie: So you miss her.

Eddie: She's a photographer, you know. Fuck her. There's pictures here. It's Hollywood.

Bonnie: Sure. You should tell her.

Eddie: Talking about love makes you feel like you're watching TV, Bonnie, that why you're so interested? *(Suddenly sitting up, startled, focusing on her.)* I'm real, Bonnie. I'm real. I'm not a goddamn TV image in front of you, here; this is real. I'm a real person, Bonnie, you know that, right? Suck my dick.

Bonnie: You know, if your manner of speech is in any way a reflection of what goes on in your head, Eddie, it's a wonder you can tie your shoes.

Eddie: You're right. You ever have that experience where your thoughts are like these totally separate, totally self-sustaining phone booths in this vast uninhabited shopping mall in your head? You ever have that experience? My inner monologue has taken on certain disquieting characteristics, I mean, I don't feel loved. Even if she loves me, I don't feel it. I don't feel loved, and I'm sick of it, you know what I mean?

Bonnie: I'm gonna go.

Eddie: What for?

Bonnie: Home. I'm going home. Maybe you been doin' too much shit, Eddie. Even outlaws have to take precautionary measures.

Eddie: Says who?

Artie and Mickey come in the door. Mickey heads up to his room, while Artie goes to the kitchen for a drink.

Mickey: Hi.

Artie: Hey.

Bonnie: I'm going home. *(Eddie is scrambling to his feet, trying to appear okay.)*

Mickey: How was your date?

Artie: We saw your date out in the bushes there like a madman. What's the haps, here, huh?

Bonnie: The hell with the bunch of you.

Eddie: He threw her out of her car. *(Staggering to the couch where he flops down.)*

Bonnie: Can't you just keep your mouth shut, Eddie? Does everybody have to know?

Eddie: Suck my dick.

Bonnie *(Heading for the door)*: Goodbye.

Artie: Whata you doin' tomorrow, Bonnie?

Bonnie: Why?

Artie: I wanna know.

Bonnie: I don't wanna tell you, it's none of your business, I'm taking my kid to Disneyland. We're goin' for the day, so I won't be home.

Eddie: You haven't been to Disneyland yet?

Bonnie: Of course we been. We been a hundred times. We like it.

Artie: I'll go with you.

Bonnie: You wanna?

Artie: Sure.

Bonnie: Great. Come by about eleven.

Artie: Okay.

Bonnie: Bye. *(As she goes out the door, Mickey comes down the stairs and crosses into the kitchen to join Artie.)*

Mickey: Bye.

Artie: Bye.

Eddie: You guys see Phil outside?

Artie: So she likes to be thrown out of cars. I threw a bitch out of bed once.

Eddie: It ain't the same thing.

Artie: Did I say it was?

Mickey: What happened?

Eddie: You implied it.

Artie: She was harassing me. We were ballin' away, she's tellin' me, "Faster, faster, slower, higher, do this, do that. Faster. Higher." So I says to her, "Hey, listen, am I in your way here, or what?" *(The front door opens, and Phil comes in carrying a baby wrapped in a blanket.)*

Phil: I got my baby.

Artie: What?

Mickey: Phil.

Phil: I got my baby.

Mickey: Whata you mean?

Phil: I went and took her.

Artie: He got his kid. You got your kid, Phil.

Mickey: Where's your wife?

Phil: Sleepin'.

Mickey: She doesn't know? *(Tentatively, Artie and Mickey move to gather around Phil and peek at the baby.)*

Phil: I snuck. I coulda been anybody. I coulda done anything. You like her?

Artie: You kidnapped her.

Phil: You want me to kill you, Artie? This is my baby here. She's mine.

Mickey: She looks like you, Phil.

Artie: Around the eyes.

Mickey: And the mouth. Look at the mouth. That's Phil's mouth.

Phil: I don't see it.

Artie: It's unmistakable.

Mickey: You don't see it in the eyes?

Phil: No, I look real hard, and I try like to think I'm looking into my own eyes, but I don't see anything of my own at all. I wish I did. Nothing familiar. Just this baby. Cute. But like I found her.

Artie: Look how she's looking at you.

Phil: They can't see. It's the sound vibrations and this big blur far away like a cloud, that's all. Wanna hold her, Eddie?

Eddie: My hands are dirty.

Phil: 'At's okay. You want her, Mickey?

Mickey: Sure.

Phil (*Carefully he passes the baby to Mickey*): She's light as a little feather, huh? You can hold her in one hand.

Artie: Does she cry?

Phil: She's very good-natured.

Mickey: What if she cries? (*Mickey, eager to get rid of the baby passes her to Eddie.*)

Artie: Tell her a joke.

Eddie *(Taking the baby)*: Ohh, she's real cute. What's happenin', little baby? Makes me miss my kid, huh?

Artie: Makes me miss my kid.

Mickey: I got two of 'em.

Eddie: This really makes me hate my ex-wife. *(Eddie laughs a little, and looks at Mickey, who laughs.)* I mean, I really hate my ex-wife. *(Now they start to make jokes, trying to break each other up, and top each other, all except, of course, Phil.)*

Artie: And this little innocent thing here, this sweet little innocent thing is a broad of the future.

Mickey: Hard to believe, huh?

Eddie: Awesome.

Artie: Depressing.

Eddie: Maybe if we kept her and raised her, she could grow up and be a decent human being.

Mickey: Unless it's just biologically and genetically inevitable that at a certain age they go nasty.

Phil: Except for the great ones.

Mickey: The great ones come along once in a lifetime.

Artie: Not in my lifetime.

Phil: Like the terrific athletes of any given generation, there's only a few.

Mickey: You think it might be wise or unwise to pay attention to the implications of what we're saying here?

Eddie: Who has time?

Mickey: Right. Who has time?

Eddie: It's hard enough to say what you're sayin', let alone to consider the goddamn implications.

Artie: Lemme see her, okay? *(As the baby is briefly in Phil's hands while on her way from Eddie to Artie, Phil stares at the child.)*

Phil: We was all that little: each one of us. I'm gonna ask Susie to give me one more try. Just one more. I'm gonna beg her.

Mickey: You oughta call her, Phil; tell her you got the kid, anyway.

Phil: I'll take the kid back. I'll beg her. I can beg.

Eddie: Phil, listen to me; you're a rare fuckin' human being. Underneath it all, you got this goddamn potential, this unbelievable potential. You really do; you could channel it.

Phil (*Unable to look at Eddie, he pulls away*): I mean, I'm startin' in my car again, Eddie. I was three days on the highway last week. Three whole days with nothing but gas station attendants. You know what I'm sayin', Eddie? I'll beg her. I'll follow her around on my hands and knees throughout the house. I won't let her out of my sight. (*Artie yelps and stares down at the baby.*) What happened?

Artie (*Hurrying to pass the baby back to her father*): She shit herself.

Mickey: Look at that smile. Ohhh, she shit herself, and look at that big smile.

Phil (*Cradling the baby*): They're very honest.

Artie: Yeah, well, she's a broad already, Phil. Just like every other broad I ever met, she hadda dump on me.

CURTAIN

Act Three

SCENE ONE

TIME: Several days later, early evening.

PLACE: The same.

Mickey and Darlene are laughing. They are at the breakfast nook counter, Mickey behind it, pouring wine, while Darlene is seated in front of it.

Mickey: All I said was "Has anybody seen him levitate?" So she says to me, "Well, he's an honest person and he has been working at it for years, so if he says he levitates, I see no reason for you to doubt it."

Darlene: Yeah, Mickey, what are you, a cynic?

Mickey: I mean, not only is she miffed at me, but the entire room is in sympathy. This is the group consensus: the guy has worked at it, so for asking a question such as, "Has anybody seen him levitate?" I'm crude. Or I don't know what.

Darlene (*Tapping his nose with her forefinger:*) Bad, bad, bad. Bad, bad.

As Mickey imitates the moans of a guilty dog, Eddie comes in through the front door and stands for a beat, looking at them.

Eddie: Bad what?

Mickey: Dog.

Darlene: Hi, honey.

Everyone, a little embarrassed, is avoiding one another's eyes.

Mickey: We were talking about that levitation guy, right?

Darlene: Which led to bad dog. Somehow.

Eddie: It would have to.

Mickey: I think it was a logical but almost untraceable sequence of associations.

Eddie: Been waiting long?

Mickey and Darlene speak almost simultaneously.

Darlene: No.

Mickey: Yeah. *(Pause.)* I have, she hasn't. I gotta go.

Eddie: Phil call?

Mickey *(Rushing about now, preparing to leave)*: Not that I know of. How's he doin'?

Eddie: I got a lot of frantic messages at work, and when I tried his house, Susie called me an "asshole" and hung up, and from then on the phone was off the hook. So much for reconciliation.

Mickey: It would appear they've found a pattern to their liking.

Darlene: I mean, Phil's a lot of fun, but on a day-to-day basis, I would have to have a lot of sympathy for Susie.

Eddie *(Heading to the kitchen and the refrigerator)*: She's a very sympathetic bitch. That's her staple attribute.

Mickey *(Near the door)*: You want me to try and hook up with you later, or you up for privacy?

Eddie: Depends on do I locate Phil or not.

Darlene: You could call, or we could leave a message.

Mickey: I'll check my service. See you. *(Mickey goes out the door.)*

Eddie: Let's just hang around a little in case he calls.

Darlene: I'm tired anyway.

Eddie: It's the kid thing, you know, that's the thing. He could walk in a second it wasn't for the kid.

Darlene: He should have then.

Eddie: Exactly. But he couldn't. *(Heading for the stairs, beginning to take off his jacket.)* So what am I talking about? It's just a guy like Phil, for all his appearances, this is what can make him nuts. You don't ever forget about 'em if you're a guy like Phil.

I mean, my little girl is a factor in every calculation I make—big or small—she's a constant. You can imagine, right?

Darlene: Sure. I had a, you know—and that was—well, rough, so I have some sense of it, really, in a very funny way.

Eddie *(As he goes into his bedroom)*: What?

Darlene: My abortion. I got pregnant. I wasn't sure exactly which guy—I wasn't going crazy or anything with a different guy every night or anything, and I knew them both very well, but I was just not emotionally involved with either one of them, seriously. *(Emerging from the bedroom, he freezes, staring down at her, his shirt half off.)* Though I liked them both. A lot. Which in a way made the whole thing even more confusing on a personal level, and you know, in terms of trying to figure out the morality of the whole thing, so I finally had this abortion completely on my own without telling anybody, not even my girlfriends. I kept thinking in my mind that it wasn't a complete baby, which it wasn't, not a fully developed person, but a fetus which it was, and that I would have what I would term a real child later, but nevertheless, I had these nightmares and totally unexpected feelings in which in my dreams I imagined the baby as this teenager, a handsome boy of real spiritual consequences, which now the world would have to do without, and he was always like a refugee, full of regret, like this treasure that had been lost in some uncalled-for way, like when a person of great potential is hit by a car. I felt I had no one to blame but myself, and I went sort of out of my mind for a while, so my parents sent me to Puerto Rico for a vacation, and I got myself back together there enough to come home with my head on my shoulders at least semi-straight. I was functional, anyway. Semi-functional, anyway. But then I told everybody what had happened. I went from telling nobody to everybody.

Eddie: This was . . .

Darlene: What?

Eddie: When?

Darlene: Seven and a half years ago.

Eddie: That's what I mean, though; those feelings.

Darlene: I know. I understood, see, that was what you meant, which was my reason for trying to make the effort to bring it up, because I don't talk about it all that much at all anymore, but I wanted you to know that when you said that about your daughter, I, in fact, in a visceral sense, knew what you were talking about.

Eddie (*Moving down the stairs toward her, as it seems they agree on everything*): I mean, everybody has this baggage, and you can't ignore it or what are you doing?

Darlene: You're just ignoring it.

Eddie: You're just ignoring the person then, that's all. But at the same time your own feelings are—it's overwhelming or at least it can be. You can't take it all on.

Darlene: No.

Eddie (*Holding her hand, he pats her in consolation*): There's nothing I can do about all that, you know, that happened to you.

Darlene: No.

Eddie: It really messed you up, though.

Darlene: For a while. But I learned certain things from it, too, you know.

Eddie (*Still holding her hand*): Sure.

Darlene: It was painful, but I learned these things that have been a help ever since, so something came out of it good.

Eddie: So . . . these two guys. . . . Where are they?

Darlene: Oh, I have no idea. This was in Cincinnati.

Eddie: Right. (*Now he rises and begins mixing drinks for them both.*)

Darlene: I don't know what happened to them. I think one got married and I have this vague sense that—I don't know what EXACTLY—but . . . No. I can't remember. But I have this sense that SOMETHING happened to him. I don't know what. Anyway, I rarely think about it anymore. I'm a very different person.

Eddie: Did . . . they know each other?

Darlene: The two guys?

Eddie: Yeah.

Darlene: No. I mean, not that I know of. Why?

Eddie: Just wondering.

Darlene: What?

Eddie: Nothing. Just . . . you know.

Darlene: You must have been wondering something. People don't just wonder nothing.

Eddie: No, no. I was just wondering, you know, was it a pattern? That's all.

Darlene: No.

Eddie: I mean, don't get irritated. You asked me.

Darlene: You asked me. I mean, I was trying to tell you something else entirely.

Eddie: I know that.

Darlene: So what's the point?

Eddie: I'm aware absolutely of what you were trying to tell me. And I heard it. But am I just supposed to totally narrow down my whole set of perceptions, just filter out everything, just censor everything that doesn't support your intention? I made an association. And it was not an unreasonable association.

Darlene: It was totally off the wall, and hostile.

Eddie: Hostile?

Darlene: And you know it.

Eddie: Give me a break! What? I'm supposed to sit still for the most arcane association I ever heard in my life, that levitation leads to dogs? But should I come up with an equally—-I mean, equally, shit—when I come up with a hundred percent more logical association, I'm supposed to accept your opinion that it isn't?

Darlene: No, no, no.

Eddie: Well, that's all it was. An association. That's all it was.

Darlene: Okay.

Eddie: I mean, for everybody's good, it appeared to me a thought worth some exploration, and if I was wrong, and I misjudged, then I'm sorry.

Darlene: It's just something I'm very, sometimes, sensitive about.

Eddie: Sure. What? The abortion.

Darlene: Yeah.

Eddie (*Handing her the drink, he pats her hand*): Sure. Okay, though? You okay now? You feel okay?

Darlene: I'm hungry. You hungry?

Eddie: I mean, if we don't talk these things out, we'll just end up with all this, you know, unspoken shit, following us around. You wanna go out and eat? Let's go out. What are you hungry for? How about Chinese?

Darlene: Sure.

Eddie (*Grabbing up the phone and starting to dial*): We could go to Mr. Chou's. Treat ourselves right.

Darlene: That's great. I love the seaweed.

Eddie: I mean, you want Chinese?

Darlene: I love Mr. Chou's.

Eddie: We could go some other place. How about Ma Maison?

Darlene: Sure.

Eddie (*Hanging up the phone*): You like that better than Mr. Chou's?

Darlene: I don't like it better, but it's great. Which one is your preference?

Eddie: Well, I want—you know—this should be—I'd like this to be your choice.

Darlene: It doesn't matter to me.

Eddie: Which one should I call?

Darlene: Surprise me.

Eddie: I don't want to surprise you. I want to, you know, do whatever you say.

Darlene: Then just pick one. Call one. Either.

Eddie: I mean, why should I have to guess? I don't want to guess. Just tell me. I mean, what if I pick the wrong one?

Darlene: You can't pick the wrong one. Honestly, Eddie, I like them both the same. I like them both exactly the same.

Eddie: Exactly?

Darlene: Yes. I like them both.

Eddie: I mean, how can you possibly think you like them both the same? One is French and one is Chinese. They're different. They're as different as—I mean, what is the world, one big blur to you out there in which everything that bears some resemblance to something else is just automatically put at the same level in your hierarchy, for chrissake, Darlene, the only thing they have in common is that they're both restaurants!

Darlene: Are you aware that you're yelling?

Eddie: My voice is raised for emphasis, which is a perfectly legitimate use of volume. Particularly when, in addition, I evidently have to break through this goddamn cloud in which you are obviously enveloped in which everything is just this blur totally void of the most rudimentary sort of distinction.

Darlene: Just call the restaurant, why don't you?

Eddie: Why are you doing this?

Darlene: I'm hungry. I'm just trying to get something to eat before I faint.

Eddie: The fuck you are. You're up to something.

Darlene: What do you mean, what am I up to? You're telling me I don't know if I'm hungry or not? I'm hungry!

Eddie: Bullshit!

Darlene (*Leaping up from her chair, she strides across the room*): "Up to?" Paranoia, Eddie. Para-fucking-noia. Be alert. Your tendencies are coming out all over the place.

Eddie: I'm fine.

Darlene (*Pacing near the base of the stairs*): I mean, to stand there screeching at me about what-am-I-up-to is paranoid.

Eddie: Not if you're up to something, it's not.

Darlene: I'm not. Take my word for it, you're acting a little nuts.

Eddie: I'm supposed to trust your judgment of my mental stability? I'm supposed to trust your evaluation of the nuances of my sanity? You can't even tell the difference between a French and a Chinese restaurant!

Darlene: I like them both.

Eddie: But they're different. One is French, and the other is Chinese. They are totally fucking different.

Darlene: Not in my inner, subjective, emotional experience of them.

Eddie: The tastes, the decors, the waiters, the accents. The fucking accents. The little phrases the waiters say. And they yell at each other in these whole totally different languages, does none of this make an impression on you?

Darlene: It impresses me that I like them both.

Eddie: Your total inner emotional subjective experience must be THIS EPIC FUCKING FOG! I mean, what are you on, some sort of dualistic trip and everything is in twos and you just can't tell which is which so you're just pulled taut between them on this goddamn high wire between people who might like to have some kind of definitive reaction from you in order to know!

Darlene: Fuck you!

Eddie: What's wrong with that?

Darlene: Is that what this is all about? Those two guys. I happened to mention two guys!

Eddie: I just want to know if this is a pattern. Chinese restaurants and you can't tell the difference between people. *(They stand, staring at each other.)*

Darlene: Oh, Eddie. Oh, Eddie, Eddie.

Eddie: What?

Darlene: Oh, Eddie, Eddie. *(Moving to the couch, she slumps down, sits there.)*

Eddie: What?

Darlene: I just really feel awful. This is really depressing. I really like you. I really do.

Eddie: I mean . . .

Darlene: What?

Eddie: Well, don't feel too bad, okay?

Darlene: I do, I feel bad. I feel bad.

Eddie *(Moving now, he sits down on the edge of the armchair, and leans toward her)*: But, I mean, just—we have to talk about these things, right? That's all. This is okay.

Darlene: No, no.

Eddie: Just don't—you know, on the basis of this, make any sort of grand, kind of overwhelming, comprehensive, kind of, you know, totally conclusive assessment here. That would be absurd, you know. I mean, this is an isolated, individual thing here, and—

Darlene: No.

Eddie *(Moving to the couch, he tries to get close to her, settles on his knees on the floor beside the couch)*: Sure. I mean, sometimes what is it? It's stuff, other stuff; stuff under stuff, you're doing one thing you think it's something else. I mean, it's always there, the family thing, the childhood thing, it's—sometimes it comes up. I go off. I'm not even where I seem anymore. I'm not there.

Darlene: Eddie, I think I should go.

Eddie: I'm trying to explain.

Darlene *(Sliding away from him)*: I know all about it.

Eddie: Whata you know all about?

Darlene: Your fucking childhood, Eddie. You tol' me.

Eddie: Whata you know?

Darlene: I know all I—what is this, a test? I mean, I know: Your parents were these religious lunatics, these pious frauds, who periodically beat the shit out of you.

Eddie: They weren't just religious, and they didn't just—

Darlene: Your father was a minister, I know.

Eddie: What denomination?

Darlene: Fuck you. *(She bolts away, starts gathering up her things: She's going to leave.)*

Eddie: You said you knew.

Darlene: I don't think there's a lot more we ought to, with any, you know, honesty, allow ourselves in the way of bullshit about our backgrounds to exonerate what is our just plain mean behavior to one another.

Eddie: That's not what I'm doing.

Darlene: So, what are you doing?

Eddie *(Following her)*: They took me in the woods; they prayed and then they beat the shit out of me; they prayed and beat me with sticks. He talked in tongues.

Darlene: She broke your nose and blacked your eyes, I know.

Eddie: Because I wanted to watch *Range Rider* on TV, and she considered it a violent program. *(Phone rings.)* So she broke my nose. That's insane.

Darlene: But I don't care, Eddie. I don't care. *(She's really ready to go now.)*

Eddie: Whata you mean?

Darlene: I mean, it doesn't matter. *(She steps for the door.)*

Eddie: It doesn't matter? What are you talking about? *(Grabbing her by the arm to detain her.)*

Darlene: It doesn't.

Eddie: No, no, no. *(As he grabs up the phone and yells into it.)* Hold on. *(Clutching Darlene in one hand and the phone in the other, he turns to her.)* No, no; it matters, and you care. What you mean is, it doesn't make any difference. *(Releasing her, he speaks into the phone.)* Hello.

Darlene: I can't stand this goddamn semantic insanity anymore, Eddie—I can't be that specific about my feelings—I can't. Will you get off the phone!

Eddie *(Into the phone)*: What? Oh, no. No, no. Oh, no.

Darlene: What?

Eddie *(Into phone)*: Wait there. There. I'll come over. *(He hangs up and stands.)*

Darlene: Eddie, what? You look terrible. What? *(He starts toward the front door.)* Eddie, who was that? What happened? Eddie!

Eddie: Phil's dead.

Darlene: What?

Eddie: Car. Car.

Darlene: Oh, Eddie, Eddie.

Eddie: What?

Darlene: I'm so sorry.

Eddie gives her a look and goes, and as he leaves her alone in the room, "Someone to Watch Over Me" sung by Willie Nelson starts to play.

BLACKOUT

The music continues.

SCENE TWO

TIME: Several days later. Evening.

PLACE: The same.

In the dark "Someone to Watch Over Me" continues. Mickey, Artie and Eddie come in through the front door. They wear dark suits. Eddie is carrying a stack of mail. As Mickey turns on the lights, the music goes out.

Artie: So now what? *(Eddie walks to the kitchen, where he stands sorting the mail, while Mickey, oddly buoyant, straightens up the room a little.)*

Mickey: I'm beat. What's his name, his agent, wasn't there. You see him?

Artie: He's an asshole. *(Settling into the swivel stool at the counter.)* He probably would have gone berserk to be at Phil's funeral. I was almost berserk.

Mickey: So it was just as well he didn't come.

Artie: Fuck him. There's no excuse.

Mickey: Funerals aren't for everybody, Artie. You know. Life . . . isn't for everybody. As Phil demonstrated. Life wasn't for him. *(Moving behind the counter, he empties an ashtray in the waste can.)*

Artie: You think he meant it?

Mickey: As much as he meant anything. How you doin'?

Artie: I'm okay. Except I feel, though, somewhat like at any moment I could turn into a hysterical like, you know, rabbit.

Mickey: Yeah. What would that be like?

Artie: I think I'm gonna go home. I think I'm gonna go home, Eddie. What time is it? I'm whipped.

Mickey: Ten twenty . . . two.

Artie: Ten? Ten? It feels like goddamn four in the morning. I feel like I been awake for years.

Mickey: It's ten twenty-two.

Artie: It is, isn't it. My watch is stopped. What happened to my watch? I'm whipped. It takes it out of you, huh, Eddie, a day like this.

Mickey: Death . . . takes it out of you?

Artie: Yeah.

Eddie: What you gonna do tomorrow?

Artie: I got a bunch of meetings. We got a development deal.

Eddie: Yeah?

Artie: Set, too. On paper. Good terms; very good terms. Terms I'm totally overjoyed about. *(There is an echo in this of their first act scene: Artie is aggressive and positive here; he is not going to let Eddie get at him again.)*

Eddie *(Smiling)*: Come by, okay?

Artie: Sure. Late. *(Starting for the door.)*

Eddie: Whatever.

Artie: Take care, you guys.

Mickey: You, too, Artie. Fuck him, huh?. *(At the door, Artie hesitates, glances back.)*

Artie: The jerk-off. *(He goes.)*

Mickey, crossing behind Eddie, pats him lightly on the back.

Mickey: How you doin', Edward?

Eddie: I don't know. You?

Mickey: Okay. *(Starting for the stairs.)*

Eddie: Oh, I'm okay. I mean, I'm okay. Is that what you're as-kin'?

Mickey: Yeah.

Eddie: Yeah, shit. I'm okay.

Mickey: Good.

As Mickey climbs the stairs, Eddie freezes and stands staring at a letter.

Eddie: Holy Jesus holy Christ, I got a letter. Phil. Phil.

Mickey: What?

Eddie *(Tearing open the letter)*: Yeah.

Mickey: What's it say? *(Coming to the stairway rail to stare down at Eddie.)*

Eddie: What? WHAT? *(Reads.)* "The guy who dies in an acci-dent understands the nature of destiny. Phil."

Mickey: What?

Eddie: That's what it says. *(Handing the letter up through the rails to Mickey, Eddie is examining the envelope.)* It's postmarked—the—this is the day. He mailed it on the day.

Mickey *(Staring at the letter)*: "The guy who dies in an accident understands the nature of destiny."

Eddie: To die in—what the fuck? I mean, Mickey, what, what, what?

Mickey *(With a shrug)*: It's a fucking fortune cookie. *(He hands the letter back down to Eddie who takes it.)*

Eddie: I mean, if he killed himself, this is the note.

Mickey: Whata you mean "if"?

Eddie: I'm giving him the benefit of the doubt. *(Sitting back against the swivel chair to intently study the letter.)*

Mickey: Eddie, c'mon, you wanna look this thing in the eye. You don't do a hundred down that narrow crease in the high ground because you're anxious to get home. A hundred MPH down Mulholland on a star-filled night is not the way to longevity. The guy behaved often, and finally, like some, you know, soulful jerk-off. Fuck him and forget him. What more can I say. *(He starts for his room.)*

Eddie: I'm gonna look up the words. *(Standing up, he heads for the stairway.)*

Mickey: What?

Eddie: On the thing here, I'm gonna see if the dictionary might help.

Mickey *(As Eddie comes running up the stairs)*: Look up the words? Are you out of your mind? Don't get involved in this thing. Don't waste your time.

Eddie: But this is it—this is what he wanted to tell us. *(Eddie goes into his bedroom.)*

Mickey: He had somethin' to say he could a give us a phone call; he could have stopped by; our door was open. He wants to get some information to me now, he's going to have to bridge the gap directly; he's going to have to make an appearance, difficult as it might be. *(Eddie, carrying a dictionary, comes out of the bedroom.)* Listen to me: Stay away from this shit. He's dead: He didn't want to discuss it before, I don't want to discuss it after. *(He grabs the dictionary from Eddie's hands.)* He had enough to keep him goin', Eddie—the wife, the kid, the career was decent—blah, blah, blah—but he had some secrets and he kept 'em, they ate a hole in his brain where his self-restaint might have been, his sense of proportion might have lingered, and without that—

Eddie *(Grabbing the dictionary back)*: But that's exactly what I'm talking about—this is the clue. To something. Maybe why. I want to know why. *(And Eddie heads down the stairs with Mickey rushing after him.)*

Mickey: What why? There's no why in a disaster like this. You know, the earth moved. He was in the wrong place; this big hole opens up, what's he gonna do?

Eddie: Your attitude, Mickey—will you please examine your fucking attitude?

Mickey: This is a dead end is all I'm saying. There's no traffic with this thing. You go in, you don't come out. The guy made a decision beyond communication.

Eddie (*Waving the note at Mickey, who grabs it*): He left a note.

Mickey: The note is tangential. It's part of his goof, you know, that he was a rational human being, when he wasn't. (*Balling up the note, he throws it on the floor.*) I want no part of this fucking, beyond-the-grave extension of his jerk-off sensibility.

Eddie (*Grabbing the note up protectively, he smooths it out on the kitchen counter in preparation to study it*): The note is what he wanted us to think.

Mickey: Bullshit.

Eddie: He left it.

Mickey: To drive us nuts from long distance. Lemme see that—what is this?

Mickey grabs the note and paces around while Eddie, sitting on the the swivel chair on the living room side of the counter, focuses on the dictionary.

Eddie: I'm gonna look up the words.

Mickey: It's a fucking fortune cookie. What's to look up? "A guy who." That's him. "Dies." In case we didn't know, he gave us a demonstration. "Accident" is to propel yourself into a brief but unsustainable orbit, and then attempt to land in a tree on the side of a cliff-like incline. "Understand" is what he had no part of. "Nature" is the tree, and "destiny" is, if you're him, you're an asshole.

Eddie (*He is busily turning pages in the dictionary*): Look. Count the letters.

Mickey: What?

Eddie: Count the words and the letters, I want to know how many letters.

Mickey: Eddie, this is dementia, here. You've flipped a circuit. Grief has put you out of order.

Eddie: You never heard of an anagram?

Mickey: Sure.

Eddie: So maybe it's an anagram.

Mickey: You think this is an anagram?

Eddie: I'd like to find out.

Mickey: You think this is an anagram?

Eddie (*Leaping up, Eddie grabs Mickey by the arm and marches him to the armchair where he sits Mickey down, handing him a pencil*): You don't have to have any faith in the fucking thought, but just as a favor, you know, participate, okay. Help me move it along. That's all I'm asking. And keep your sarcasm to yourself.

Mickey: What sarcasm?

Eddie (*Getting back to the counter, the dictionary*): Can you do that?

Mickey: What sarcasm? I'm—you know—this is—What sarcasm? This is insulting.

Eddie: You're getting sidetracked.

Mickey: I'll do this goddamn lunacy. I'll count the letters here, but get one thing straight, all right? There's no sarcasm here. (*He is so irritated, he cannot stay seated. He's up, he's down, dropping the pencil, picking it up, he steps toward Eddie, then back to the armchair.*) I've indulged in nothing even remotely sarcastic here, and I want that understood because you have obviously not understood it. So I'll make allowances, but if I've been flip, it's to put some humor into what could be totally and utterly morbid—and there have been times in the goddamn history of mankind where a little humor won a person some affection for the effort, you know, not to go under; anybody can go under. I mean, we're all goin' fuckin' under, so how about a little laugh along the way? So I'm flip. So what!

Eddie: I don't feel like being flip.

Mickey: Right. But you wanna do a goddamn anagram, right? On his death note. Whata you expect to uncover, the buried treasure of his mid-life crisis, and how it might hope to be viewed retrospectively? Fine. I'll give you a hand, but if you think there's blood in this stone, man, just forget about it.

Eddie: "Flip" IS "sarcastic," Mickey.

Mickey (*Rising, starting to cross toward Eddie*): It is not. It's— "flip." On a whole other level, a whole other lower level and just lighter.

Eddie: To me, it's "sarcastic." (*Eddie is bowed over the dictionary, his fingers marking pages as Mickey, carrying the note comes up behind him.*)

Mickey: But that's crazy! Sarcastic is "heavy." It's mean. Funny, sure, but mean. I do both, but this was flip.

Eddie: You shoulda heard yourself.

Mickey: I did.

Eddie: You shoulda listened closer.

Mickey: You wanna get on with this. (*He crosses around to the kitchen side of the counter and flops into the other swivel chair, starting to pour himself a drink.*) So whata you got there?

Eddie (*Reading from the dictionary*): So I have "accident" here, and "destiny." "Accident: a happening that is not expected, foreseen or intended. Two, an unfortunate occurrence or mishap, sudden fall, collision, usually resulting in physical injury." Blah-blah, just repeats basically. And "destiny," we have, "The inevitable or necessary succession of events. What will necessarily happen to any person or thing." So, if you die in a happening that is not expected, foreseen or intended, you understand the inevitable or necessary succession of events.

Mickey: Fuck him. (*He tosses the note into the trash can.*)

Eddie: It makes sense.

Mickey (*Moving off toward the couch and TV*): It makes no sense.

Eddie (*Following Mickey*): I mean, we owe him to understand as best we can what he wanted. Nobody has to believe it.

Mickey: Anyway, he did it on purpose, so it was no goddamn accident. *(Sitting down on the couch, Mickey grabs the* TV Guide*):* And if it was no accident, then his note is categorically, definitively irrelevant.

Eddie *(Sinking onto the edge of the armchair, squeezing the dictionary, looking at Mickey):* But how did he get there? Exactly how did he get to that point where in his own mind he could do it on purpose? That's what—

Mickey: It's not that big a deal—that's the fucking truth, you know, you make an adjustment, that's all—you shift your point a view a little and what was horrible looks okay. All the necessary information that might deter you gets locked away. Little gremlins divert the good thoughts so you don't hear them. You just hear the bad thoughts, which at this point are convincing you they're a good idea. *(Rising, loosening his tie, taking off his jacket, Mickey moves toward the kitchen.)* You get an idea, that's all. You don't understand the scope of it; you just lose the scope of it. So there you are, foot's on the gas, you're flying. So far so good. No big deal. Road, trees, radio. What's a little flick of the steering wheel? Maybe an inch's rotation. Nothing to it. An inch, what's that? So you do it. *(From the cabinets he grabs a bowl and a box of Cheerios.)* But with that, what? You've gone beyond what you can come back from. You've handed control over now, it's gravity and this big machine, which is a car, who are in charge now. Only it's not a car anymore. It's this hunk of metal rearranging itself according to the laws of physics, force and reaction, stress and resistance; heat, friction, collapse, and then you're gone, who knows where. *(With a shrug, he heads triumphantly for the refrigerator to get some milk.)*

Eddie: So how many letters?

Mickey: Right. The fucking anagram. This is exciting, Eddie; I've never been involved with a being from another planet before. *(Picking the crumpled note from the trash can, he tosses it toward Eddie.)* Twelve and fifty-four. *(The note lands on the floor, and Mickey pours milk on his cereal.)*

Eddie: Twelve words and fifty-four letters. That's interesting. *(Picking up the note.)*

Mickey: It's interesting, huh?

Eddie (*With the note and dictionary, he settles on the floor, making a little desk of the coffee table*): Don't you see?

Mickey (*Standing behind the counter, he eats*): You're in charge here, Eddie.

Eddie: But don't you see?

Mickey: Yes. I almost see.

Eddie: I mean, they're both even. For one thing. There's lots of relationships.

Mickey: Can I ask you something?

Eddie: Sure. No!

Mickey: I can't?

Eddie: No.

Mickey: How ripped are you?

Eddie: I don't have time for your question. (*Furious, Eddie rises up on his knees.*) You can make a worthwhile contribution to this project here, or you can forget about it, but your animosity, or whatever it is—resistance—it's nothing but static. I need some goddamn support and you're delivering all this—whatever it is. I mean, give me a break.

Mickey: Common sense.

Eddie (*Advancing on Mickey, carrying the dictionary and note*): Is that what you think you're going to talk me into? Like what, for example, based on your vast experience with common sense is the take on this?

Mickey: It happens.

Eddie (*Something wild is entering into Eddie as he faces Mickey across the counter*): "It happens?" On a friend's death, you absolutely ransack the archives of your whole thing and come up with "It happens." (*As it appears Eddie is now going to work on the counter, Mickey grabs a* Daily Variety *and starts away.*) You need some help, Mickey. Common sense needs some help.

Mickey *(Moving with his* Daily Variety *to the couch, he flops down to read)*: You need some sleep.

Eddie *(Working at the counter)*: I mean, I think if he did it this way, if it is an anagram, it wouldn't be cryptic. The cryptic element would have been, you know, more than handled by the fact that it was in a fucking anagram to begin with, right?

Mickey *(Reading)*: Sure.

Eddie: I mean, that makes sense, right?

Mickey *(Turning a page)*: Absolutely.

Eddie: Mickey, for crissake, have all the goddamn private disdain you want in reserve, but follow the logic of what I'm saying. It's logical.

Mickey *(Glancing up)*: I'm in total fucking agreement. Anagram would more than handle cryptic.

Eddie: I tried to warn him, you know. She was a snake. And I tried to tell him, you know, she was out to absolutely undermine the little faith he had in himself. I saw it coming; she hadda see it coming. I mean, for all his toughness, he was made out of thin air, he was a pane of glass, and if you went near him, you knew it. I'm gonna call her. *(Whirling, Eddie reaches for the phone.)*

Mickey: Who? Susie? *(Rushing to the phone to stop Eddie.)* Eddie, you don't know what you're doing. You can't call her up in the middle of the night; she's a widow. She just put her husband in the ground.

Eddie: I want her to have some fucking cognizance of this event.

Mickey: She knows.

Eddie: She killed him? You ain't sayin' she's looking at it from the context she killed him?'

Mickey: What?

Eddie: You bet you're not because what she knows is he's dead and that's how much better than him she is. No more teddy bears—she's takin' care of business, so she's a together bitch, and he's weak, he punked out. A person cannot keep up their self-respect they know they look like some goddamn crazed insensitive prick who goes around dropping kids out of his life like they're trash to him. I saw it in him. She should have. What the hell was she thinking about?

Mickey: Herself. I don't know. What do people think about?

Eddie: Fuck her. What's she got to think about?

Mickey: She wanted things. I don't know. So she thought about the things she wanted. You want to kill her for what she was doing—to get things she wanted. You can't kill people for that.

Eddie *(Grabbing his box of dope and coke from its shelf under the counter)*: She killed him.

Mickey: You're gonna die a this shit, Eddie. Does it not cross your mind?

Eddie: Hey, don't get serious here, Mickey. You know, don't get morbid here and ruin a nice evening. *(Spreading his vials out on the counter.)* Die of it is a little extreme. You have to admit that. And even if it isn't, take care of myself for what? For some state-of-the-art bitch to get her hooks into me. They're fucking ghouls, Mickey. They eat our hearts.

Mickey: You don't know what you're saying. You don't. *(Pouring a large glass of vodka.)*

Eddie: I do.

Mickey *(Moving restlessly with his vodka and* Variety, *not quite knowing where to go, he ends up perched then on the edge of the big armchair)*: I know what you think you're saying, but you're not saying it.

Eddie: I do. I do. I know what I'm saying. I don't know what I mean, but I know what I'm saying. Is that what you mean?

Mickey: Yeah.

Eddie *(Snorting a line of coke off the kitchen counter)*: Right. But who knows what anything means, though, huh? It's not like anybody knows that, so at least I know I don't know, which is more than most people. They probably think they know what they mean, not just what they think they mean. You feel that, Mickey, huh? *(He starts to move around behind Mickey, coming up on his right side.)* About death, that when it comes, you're just going along in this goddamn ongoing inner rapateta, rapateta, blah-blah-blah, in which you understand this or that, and tell yourself about it, and then you ricochet on, and then it just cuts out—mid-something. Mid-realization. "Oh, now I under—" Blam! You're gone. Wham! Comatose. Dead. You think that's how it is? *(Ending up close to Mickey's head, stretched around the armchair, whispering into Mickey's right ear.)*

Mickey: I'm going to bed. *(He stands and takes a gulp of vodka.)* And you should, too. Go to bed. You're a mess. Phil would want you to get your rest.

Eddie: Fuck you about him, Mickey. *(Getting to his feet.)* I mean, where do you get the goddamn cynicism, the goddamn scorn to speak his name, let alone—

Mickey: Eddie, Eddie, is everything my fault?

Eddie: What'd you ever do but mock him and put him down?

Mickey: Relent, I beg you.

Eddie *(Advancing on Mickey)*: You ain't saying you ever did one good thing for him, are you, not one helpful thing!?

Mickey: No, Eddie, what I'm saying is that unlike you, I never lied to him.

Eddie *(Trapping Mickey against the counter)*: And you never loved him either.

Mickey: Right, Eddie. Good taste has no doubt deprived me of a great many things. *(Slipping free now, Mickey glides behind the counter to get a drink.)*

Eddie: You lie to yourself, Mickey.

Mickey: Who better?

Eddie: No guts. No originality; no guts. *(He moves toward the couch, as Mickey, behind the counter is furiously pouring himself some vodka in a water glass.)*

Mickey: You want this goddamn ultra-modern, post-hip, comprehensive, totally fucking cost-efficient explanation of everything by which you uncover the preceding events which determined the following events, but you're not gonna find it. *(And Mickey takes a drink.)*

Eddie: Says you.

Mickey: You wanna believe that if you do or don't do certain things now, certain other things will or won't happen down the road, accordingly. You think you're gonna parlay this finely tuned circuitry you have for a brain into some form of major participation in the divine conglomerate, man, but all you're gonna really do is make yourself and everyone around you, nuts. *(And Mickey drinks again.)*

Eddie: Hey, I'm just tryin' to level out here, Mick—the lobes are humming, you know—I got sonar bouncing off the moon; I got—

Mickey: I mean, to whatever extent THIS FUCKING TORMENT OF YOURS is over whatshername, Darlene, believe me, she isn't worth it.

Eddie: Ohhh, that move you made when you gave her up for her own good, that was genius. Whatever prayer I might have had was gone. She had you down as some form of totally unique, altruistic phenomenon, instead of the fact that you had a low opinion of her and what you really wanted was to fuck the bubble-brain Artie had brought us.

Mickey: So what?

Eddie: You're no better off than me.

Mickey: Just slightly.

Eddie: You don't have any feelings at all.

Mickey: I don't have your feelings, Eddie; that's all. I have my own. They get me by.

Eddie: So what kind of friendship is this?

Mickey: Adequate. Goodnight. *(Turning, he starts for the stairs.)*

Eddie: Somethin' terrible is goin' on, Mickey. It's a dark time.

Mickey: People been sayin' that since the beginning of time, Eddie. Don't feel particularly put upon, okay. Forget about it.

Eddie: That doesn't mean forget about it. That just means it's been going on a long time.

Mickey (*At the top of the stairs, he turns to look down*): I mean, Eddie, it's not the time that's dark, it's just you. You know? It's just you.

Eddie (*A mix of fury and scorn*): C'mon, scumbag, where you goin'? We'll rant at the tube.

Mickey: No.

Eddie: The tube, the tube—it's the asshole of our times. You'll love it.

Mickey: Wait up for Phil, why don't you? Wouldn't that be great if Phil came by? To keep you company. I'm sure he will. He always did.

Eddie (*Turning on the TV and getting, instantly* The Tonight Show, *the intro music loud*): I can't hear you, Mickey. I got the tube. The tube and twenty-seven cable channels. I'm set for life.

Mickey: Goodnight. (*Mickey goes toward his bedroom door.*)

Eddie: The tube. The tube. The best and brightest predigested. The dream devoured and turned to incandescent shit. (*Mickey's door slams.*) Fuck you, Mickey. All right. All right. I'm on my own. (*He starts talking to Johnny Carson on the TV.*) How you doin', huh, John? (*Rushes to the counter, his coke vial in his hand. Behind the counter, he pulls out booze bottles, several joints and then a bunch of vials of pills.*) Hey, Carson! Hey, you motherfucker, huh? It's you and me, that's right. Head to head. Eyeball to eyeball, John. And I am fortified. (*Holding up his various drugs and vials.*) Here's for my left lobe. Here's for my right lobe. And here's to keep the spark plugs blasting. (*From the TV, the audience is shouting "Yo" to Johnny.*) Yo! Yo! (*Johnny announces that this is* The Tonight Show's *19th anniversary.*) Your anniversary! Oh, my god. Your anniversary! No, you didn't get my card because I didn't send you a fucking card, John! (*Johnny says that Ed looks like a "large penguin," as Eddie at the counter begins sorting pills from vials; he drops pills into a large water glass.*) Penguins? You think that's funny? Bullshit! Funny is your friends disappearing down roads and hallways. Out of cars and behind closed doors. We got a skull in our skin, John, and we got ghosts. That's funny. (*John talks about "foreplay."*) Foreplay? Foreplay? Grow up! They're talking about quarks. They want us to think about quarks. They're going to teach our children about quarks. And Black Holes. Imagine that. Black holes, John. The heavens. Astronauts. Men in—OH! (*Suddenly remembering.*) This morning, John, there was this guy—(*Running to the TV, carrying his glass of pills and a bottle of booze, which he sets down*)—Oh, you want funny? This one'll put you away, John— (*Grabbing up the newspaper.*) We got this guy on the obit page— he WAS an astronaut, who went round the moon and ended up in Congress and had surgery for a malignancy in his nose, then passed away six months later. (*Having rummaged in the paper, he now finds the page.*) I know, I know, it's touchy material, John, but it's rich, it's ripe, you'll love it. His campaign slogan was, "I was privileged to be one of the few who viewed our earth from the moon, and that vision taught me that technology and commitment can overcome any challenge." Here's a guy who went into orbit; he rendezvoused with the moon, and from that vantage what most impressed him was HIS OWN ABILITY TO GET THERE! Hovering in the heavens, what he saw was the MAGNIFICENCE OF MEN AND MACHINES! HE MIGHT AS WELL HAVE BEEN IN DETROIT. Right? And if technology and commitment are the instruments to overcome any challenge, I want to ask him, what about his nose?! (*Laughter from the TV. The front door is slowly opened, as Donna comes in, fearfully, quite slowly. She stares at Eddie, ranting at the TV. She looks around and sneaks closer, moving along behind the couch to see what he's looking at. She is heavily made up, her clothing in disarray, and tattered, her makeup old and smeared in some places.*) I know, I know, I could have crossed the boundary here of discretion. It's possible: my own sense of discrimination has taken quite a blast. I've been humbled, John. I been blasted. And I mean, I'm not tryin' to make a finished thing here, just rough in a couple of ideas. You could refine 'em, put your stable on 'em. Right? *(He takes a huge drink of vodka.)* Right, John?? You're not listening to me. You never listen to me. *(He is hitting the TV with a newspaper. Donna has been reaching to touch him, to get his attention.)* You never listen to me! *(And now her hand hits his shoulder. He jumps. She jumps back, moving backwards so she ends up in front of him.)*

Donna: Hey, Eddie! I ain't mad anymore. You mad? See my, ah, you know, outfit? I got a little bit from everywhere I been so I'm like my own, you know, whatchamacallit. Right? Bits and pieces. So you can look at me and get the whole picture. See— here's Florida. *(She points to a patch on her clothes.)* And here's Vermont. *(Another patch.)* Which is a New England state. So if you put it together with a little thought, you can see I hitch-hiked up and down the entire East Coast.

Eddie: Unless you took a plane.

Donna: Oh, no. I didn't. Airplane? Where would I get the money? How you been?

Eddie: I'm a wreck.

Donna *(Hobbling a little, she leans against the armchair to pull off one shoe. She is weary; her sock is torn, her foot sore)*: You look a wreck, actually, but I didn't want to be impolite and mention it.

Eddie: I don't know what I'm doing, you know what I mean?

Donna: You're watchin' TV.

Eddie: Right.

Donna *(Tentatively, she is looking about for something to eat and drink; she is edging for the kitchen)*: I'm gonna eat something, okay?

Eddie: I don't know when I thought of you last, and in you walk. I don't get it.

Donna: I'm a surprise is all.

Eddie *(Rising, Eddie moves after her)*: But I mean, I don't know what pertains to me and what doesn't.

Donna (*A little startled by his sudden movement, she falters*): Whata you mean?

Eddie: I mean, everything. Right? I don't know what of everything going on pertains to me and what is of no account at all.

Donna: Everything pertains to you, Eddie.

Eddie: Yeah?

Donna: Sure. (*Finding a plate with leftover bread on it.*) It's all part of the flow of which we are a part, too, and everything pertains to everything one way or another, see what I mean?

Eddie: But I don't know, see, I don't KNOW.

Donna: It doesn't matter.

Eddie: So I'm just in this flow, right, like you in your elevator.

Donna (*Finding an open bottle of water*): It wasn't mine.

Eddie: So how'm I supposed to feel about it? See that's what I don't know.

Donna (*Moving to the armchair to eat*): You have total, utter, complete freedom on that score, Eddie, because it doesn't make a bit of difference.

Eddie (*Following her*): What I feel, it doesn't matter? This flow don't care!

Donna: I don't think so.

Eddie: So fuck it then! What good is it?

Donna: I don't know.

Eddie: Wait a minute, wait a minute—I don't think you know what I'm talking about. And I'm trying to grasp and, you know, incorporate as good advice what is your basic and total misunderstanding. I mean, is it pertinent, for example, that you came by?

Donna: It doesn't matter.

Eddie: I know that's what you think, but that's only because you have totally missed my point.

Donna: Oh, no. So what is it?

Eddie: I'm trying to say.

Donna: Great!

Eddie: I HAVE SO MUCH TO FIGURE OUT. *(Pacing near the TV, Eddie grabs up the newspaper.)* I mean, there's you there, and then there's other items like this and this, and does it pertain to me, FOR EXAMPLE, that I read that-my-government-is-selling - baby - milk - formula - to - foreign - countries - in - order - that - the - mothers' - milk - will - dry - up - from - lack - of - use - and - the - formula-supply—you following me so far?—the-formula-supply-is-cut-off-and-the-babies-starve. I mean, how am I supposed to feel about that? First of all, I can't even be certain that it's even true. All I can be sure of is that it's printed in this goddamn newspaper. And I can't find out. How'm I supposed to find out? Write my congressman? Hire a goddamn private detective? Bring my private life to a screeching halt and look into it? I couldn't even if I wanted to. And should I ever figure it out, how the hell do I influence the course of these things? I mean, what am I supposed to do about all these things?

Donna: I don't know.

Eddie: That's my point, that's what I'm saying.

Donna: So I do know your point.

Eddie: But do they pertain to me?

Donna: You're certainly worried about them.

Eddie: I'm aware that I'm worried about them.

Donna: I mean, I was saying to you that they all pertain to you as much as they're part of everything, right? That's what I was saying.

Eddie: But as real things or as rumors?

Donna: Whichever they are.

Eddie: Which we don't know.

Donna: Right. So this would qualify as a mystery, Eddie, right?

Eddie: Yeah.

Donna: So you can't straighten out a mystery, right? That's all I'm saying.

Eddie: Did you know Phil is dead?

Donna: Wow. What happened?

Eddie: He drove his car off Mulholland.

Donna: What happened?

Eddie: The car crashed.

Donna: No shit. I read about that. I read about that in the paper, but I didn't recognize his name, even though it was the same name.

Eddie: Funeral was today.

Donna: Wow. So that's why you're such a wreck, Eddie. No wonder. You were at the funeral.

Eddie: Yeah.

Donna: That'd wreck anybody.

Eddie: Yeah.

Donna: Was it sad?

Eddie (*With a shrug, Eddie gets through it quickly, not seeming to care at all*): You know, everybody wears the suits, you do the things. Everybody's there; you hang around, you know. The cars. Everybody gets to the church. So the priest is there, he blah-blah, blah-blah-blah, some guy is singing, mmmmmmmmmmmmnnnnnnnnnn, mmmmm, you drive to the cemetery, right. Everybody's in a line, cars all in a line. Brrrmmmm, brrrrrrmmmm. Everybody's in the cars; blah-blah, blah-blah-blah. So we get to the cemetery, the priest's got some more to say, rapateta, rapateta. So there's the hole, put him in. Blah-blah, blah-blah-blah.

Donna: Was it sad?

Eddie (*Somewhere, here it hits him, a grief that, though there are tears, is beyond them: It is in his body, which heaves, and wracks him*):

There was in the church we were all like a bunch of dogs. This guy would sing with his beautiful voice. He had this beautiful high voice. All alone. No organ or anything. Just his voice. And we would all start to cry. The priest could say anything, a lot a nice things; sad things. Nothin'. But then this guy from way in the back of the church would sing, and you couldn't hear the words even, just this high, beautiful, sad sound, this human sound, and we would all start to cry along with him. (*He gasps, tries to breathe.*)

Donna: You know somethin', Eddie. I didn't really go to all these actual places on my clothes.

Eddie: No.

Donna: No. (*Moving closer to him.*) I thought about them all though, and bought the souvenirs at a local souvenir place, and I dreamed these big elaborate dreams about these places. First, I would buy this book all about these places like Lauderdale, and Miami and Boston, and then I knew what I was dreaming about, and I could dream with accurate and convincing details, but actually I went out of here north toward San Francisco, but I got no further than Oxnard.

Eddie (*Sitting up, trying to get himself under control*): I know where Oxnard is.

Donna (*With immense enthusiasm*): Great!

Eddie (*Laughing a little*): What's so great about me knowing where Oxnard is?

Donna: It's great when people know what each other are talking about, right, isn't that what we been talking about? I fell in love with a Mexican there. But after a while it wasn't love.

Eddie: What was it?

Donna: A mess. So I'm gonna sleep here if you don't mind. You got room?

Eddie: I'm gonna be up for a while.

Donna (*Standing up, looking around*): Oh, I don't care. I'm just happy to get off the streets at the moment. The desperation out there is paranormal.

Eddie: I don't know if I'm going to sleep ever again. I might stay awake forever.

Donna: That's okay; should I lay down on the floor?

Eddie: No, there's room here.

Eddie slides to one end of the couch, while Donna, carrying her coat, settles in against him, covering herself with her coat, then she looks up at him.

Donna: You wanna fuck me or anything, Eddie, before I go to sleep?

Eddie: No.

Donna: Great. Not that I don't want to, I'm just sleepy.

Eddie: You want a lude, or anything?

Donna: No. *(Turning back to go to sleep.)*

Eddie: Valium?

Donna: No. 'Night.

Eddie: Goodnight.

Donna: Pleasant dreams.

He holds her.

BLACK OUT

CURTAIN

AFTERWORD

by David Rabe

The fact that I write a play with only the slightest premeditation regarding its intentions and implications, and then come through the simple passage of time along with the process of rehearsal and study to an intense and extensive understanding of the completed play's subterranean nature and needs, and that I am then devoted to the expression of these themes with a fanatical ardor, is a continual experience of amazement for me.

I remember beginning *Hurlyburly* with an impulse that took its shape, at least partly, in a mix of feelings spawned in my own experiences and also from my observations of the prices some men were paying from within their varied armored and defended stances—the current disorientation and accompanying anger many feel at having been flung out from the haven of their sexual and marital contexts and preconceptions. Whether they were right or wrong was not at all my concern, but the fact that they had been raised in a certain manner with certain obligations, duties and expectations (all defined as natural) which, though they led to privilege in the social order, carried with them certain hidden but equally inevitable effects of personal and emotional self-distortion, a crippling. Around me, and within myself, I felt I saw the wild reactions of creatures who had been recently given the good news that they had brutalized large portions of themselves for a disreputable cause, and now, if only they would quickly change, they would find fulfillment. Trained to control their feelings and think, they must now stop thinking and feel. Having been trained to be determined, hard, and dominant, they must now swoon into the ecstasies of submission. It was a confusing melee of contradictory exhortations, a great many of which, both past

161

and present, came from women. On one hand these men had
the admonitions and codes of their childhoods, while on the
other there were their companions and contemporaries, who,
awakened by the Women's Liberation Movement, were now
pointing angrily to claim obvious rights for which they had, to
all appearances in the past, lacked all desire. In this disturbing
crunch of righteously contradictory commands, a great many
men simply recoiled or, suspecting a further treachery, grew
mean and wary or ossified defiantly, or felt that without their
gains they would vanish, or simply loved their privilege more
than what they had lost, or experienced their losses as gains.
And some of all of these, along with others who had in fact
attempted the change but ended up stranded, were sustaining
themselves with a wide variety of drugs, or spinning out into
brief but costly episodes of self-destructive frenzy, or even
dropping dead. Not that I felt that the provocations of purely
sociological change were the exclusive substance of their fates,
but this was what I knew at this point which was, as I have
stated, my crude and preliminary beginning.

A second factor in the brew was an impulse to venture near
at least the appearances of the so-called "realistic" or "well-
made" play, which in my view is that form which thinks that
cause and effect are proportionate and clearly apparent, that
people know what they are doing as they do it, and that others
react accordingly, that one thing leads to another in a rational,
mechanical way, a kind of Newtonian clock of a play, a kind of
Darwinian assemblage of detail which would then determine
the details that must follow, the substitution of the devices of
logic for the powerful sweeps of pattern and energy that is our
lives.

To start, I merely started: I wrote whatever I could, any
scene or exchange of dialogue that occurred to me with no
concern for sequence, hoping only for vitality, and believing I
would find within the things I wrote the cues for order. I remember having written much of Act One, and perhaps two
thirds of Act Two—enough to know that Phil would die—and
then I found myself at the beginning of the last scene, the re-
turn from Phil's funeral, and suddenly the dialogue pertaining
to the note and anagram began to show up.

I remember being baffled and thrilled. The content of the

note, "The guy who dies in an accident understands the nature of destiny," was in no way preplanned, and I had no idea what the dictionary would offer by way of illumination until, like Eddie, I went to it. What it gave, which is what is quoted in the play, made for me an eerie and comforting sense, however enigmatic it might appear: "If you die in a happening that is not expected, foreseen or intended, you understand the inevitable or necessary succession of events." With this discovery, which was itself an outcome of chance, the play took on an entrancing addition.

And so it proceeded: I recollect early days in rehearsal when questions were addressed to me and I had no answers. I had no knowledge as to what a character was up to or intended, or what a scene was meant to convey, and I was forced to answer from this not-knowing. And yet I had to note that as moments were worked on or characters' motives or states attempted or discussed, I would have a strong sense of what was not correct, and occasionally, as time went on and our process took us to Chicago, I began to possess a certainty or two about what a character was or wanted as opposed to merely knowing what he wasn't or what it was he didn't want.

In the beginning we all had felt that the aspects of the play which would prove difficult to contend with in rehearsal would be the male characters' feelings about the female characters, and the actors' and actresses' encounters with these feelings. However, as rehearsal progressed, what we found was that the women came in and did their work rather simply and directly and the development of their scenes progressed rather quickly. Meanwhile, the men were bickering and struggling with feelings of competitiveness and resentment, shifting alliances, hurt feelings, and a fear that the play was going to crush us all collectively and individually. In other words, the difficulty in the play was in what the men wanted from and dreaded in one another: who was boss and could anybody be trusted? Somewhere in the encounter with this experience I began to see that, certainly, there were sociological considerations in the play—evaluations of the relationships between men and women in a specific time, and a specific place (though I personally feel the Hollywood connection has been vastly over-emphasized in reactions to the play, and that this is a tactic for pushing the implications of it into some quarantined region or eccentricity—"the West Coast"—so that it need not be considered as personally pertinent). Yet beyond these contemporary observations some other set of forces was at work, and in the deeper architecture of the play the women were the thrusts of emotion, the threatening surges of the forces of feeling, as if the play were one huge personality at war with itself, filled with dread of feeling on one hand and a sense somewhere in its guts that to be in charge was only an illusion of safety, that control was in fact the enterprise of hanging mid-air in the unbuoyed substanceless claims of ego.

It was at this point that I encountered in a book I had owned for years but left unread a passage offering a Jungian interpretation of a New Testament parable:

> The King is the central authority, a symbol of the Self. He identifies himself with "the least"—that aspect of the personality which is despised and is considered to have no value. "The least" is hungry and thirsty; that is, it is the needy, desirous side of ourselves. It is a stranger, referring to that aspect which is lonely and unaccepted. It is naked, that is, exposed and unprotected. It is sick, the side of the psyche that is diseased, pathological, neurotic. And finally, it is in prison—confined and punished for some transgression of collective rules and behavior. All these aspects of the rejected shadow are equated with the "King," which means psychologically that acceptance of the shadow and compassion for the inferior inner man are equivalent to acceptance of the Self.[1]

That Eddie and Mickey were the royalty in the play had been discussed, the term "princes" often used in reference to them. And Phil obviously was "the least," needy, wild, desirous, desperate, an ex-con or prisoner and mysteriously loved by Eddie—mysteriously in the sense that there could be no easily grasped rational justification for the esteem in which he was held by Eddie. Yet if this code of "King" and "least" were taken as a key for the subterranean concerns of the play then it was

[1] Edward F. Edinger, *Ego and Archetype* (New York, G. P. Putnam's Sons, 1972), p. 144.

Eddie's affection for Phil that was, oddly enough, his highest
virtue.

Days later I encountered another paragraph in the same
book which stated:

> "To this day God is the name by which I designate all
> things which cross my willful path violently and reck-
> lessly, all things which upset my subjective views, plans
> and intentions and change the course of my life for bet-
> ter or worse."
>
> The view Jung is expressing is essentially a primitive
> view, albeit a conscious and sophisticated one. Jung is
> calling "God" what most people would call chance or ac-
> cident.[2]

Certainly this would seem a correlation and validation for the
apparently contradictory claims of Phil's note.

On each subsequent day as I observed rehearsals or per-
formances in Chicago I felt my grasp of things increase,
though never did I feel I reached a point of certain and complete comprehension. Then, after the New York opening, I
was asked to write something for a magazine, and I found myself thinking, "Alright, maybe I can. What I would like to do is
to make it clear—the heart of it—I'll write about the union of
opposites, the alchemical theme of the play, the unconscious
core."

The tone of the voice suggesting this tactic was quite angry,
I remember, bitter and rebellious for it felt the reception of the
play to date had been without any attention to such under-
tones. Yet I did nothing, and felt I would probably do nothing,
until one night I received a phone call from a friend who, having seen the play in both Chicago and New York, wanted to tell
me he had read what he felt was a description of Eddie, his
progress and state, in Jung's book *Mysterium Coniunctionis* in a
chapter entitled, "The Conjunction," which is subtitled "The
Alchemical View of the Union of Opposites."

> But if his recognition of the shadow is as complete as he
> can make it, then conflict and disorientation ensue, an
> equally strong Yes and No which he can no longer keep

---

[2] Ibid., p. 101.

apart by a rational decision. *He cannot transform his clini-
cal neurosis into the less conspicuous neurosis of cynicism*; in
other words, he can no longer hide the conflict behind
a mask. It requires a real solution and necessitates a
third thing in which the opposites can unite. Here the
logic of the intellect usually fails, for in a logical antith-
esis there can be no third. The "solvent" can only be of
an irrational nature. In nature the resolution of opposites is always an energetic process: she acts symbolically
in the truest sense of the word, doing something that
expresses both sides, just as a waterfall visibly mediates
between above and below.[3] (Emphasis added.)

Excited by a sense of relevance, I glanced about at the nearby
paragraphs and noted almost immediately something in the
preceding lines:

Such a situation is bound to arise when the analysis of
the psychic contents, of the patient's attitude and particularly of his dreams, has brought the compensatory or
complementary images from the unconscious so insis-
tently before his mind that the conflict between the conscious and the unconscious personality becomes open
and critical. When this confrontation is confined to par-
tial aspects of the unconscious the conflict is limited and
the solution simple: *the patient, with insight and some res-
ignation or a feeling of resentment, places himself on the side
of reason and convention.* Though the unconscious motifs
are repressed again, as before, the unconscious is satis-
fied to a certain extent, because the patient must now
make a conscious effort to live according to its principles
and, *in addition, is constantly reminded of the existence of the
repressed by annoying resentments.*[4] (Emphasis added.)

For me, then, exposure to the entirety of this quote along with
the others I had encountered produced a capacity in me to
speculate confidently on the dynamics at the base of the play:
there was Mickey, a figure apparently settled on the side of

---

[3] C. J. Jung, *Mysterium Coniunctionis,* trans. by R. F. C. Hill (Princeton, A
Bollingen Series, 1963), p. 495.
[4] Ibid., p. 494.

convention and reason, yet full of resentment and animosity, however veiled, against Phil who was the shadow, the prisoner, the outlaw, the ex-con of banished passions, while it was Eddie who had been carried to a recognition of "Phil" from which he could not retreat, the "Phil" in himself, the forces of vitality and disorder with which Phil was identified and to which Eddie was now drawn with an equally strong Yes and No that he could no longer control and manipulate through rational decision nor could he in the end maintain his masks as Mickey could, nor any longer find comfort in the consolations of cynicism offered by Mickey. Though Eddie might try to aid Phil to learn to control and understand himself, Mickey would ridicule the effort, seeking at every opportunity to mock or provoke Phil. And, in addition, it had to be recognized that, however much Eddie might base his relationship with Phil on a real enjoyment and love, it was also founded, at least partly if not equally, upon the belief that Phil and the powers in his realm must be channeled or they would overwhelm large and essential quantities of what Eddie thought to be himself. Where Mickey might oppose the threat of Phil with the simple tactic of rational condemnation and, by this means, keep himself well removed from any possible influence, Eddie, no longer capable of maintaining such a purely cerebral stance, was drawn toward the dangers of conflict and disorientation as if spellbound. And in this play it was the women who were most familiar with this state, and finally its fullest embodiment, for they were clearly more intimate with the spectrum of their emotional life, and lacking social station, they were to a large extent without conventional power. Yet they had their effect. For though they were brought in again and again as coins to be passed among the men, in exchanges in which it was expected of them that they would serve as pacifiers to discharge some male's high state of stress or emotion, it is certainly true that, more often than not, they confounded this function, tending quite powerfully to arouse in the men the very thing they had been brought in to diminish—a more extreme state of disruptive emotion. The immensity of the effort of the men to diminish and trivialize, categorize, and imprison the force they felt to be in the women was a measure of the fear they had of the chaos they felt to reside there—though it no doubt resided at least equally, if not predominantly within themselves, then "Phil."

Somewhere in the midst of these considerations I recollected a statement I had made quite early in rehearsal when, in an effort to articulate what the overall pattern of the play was, I said that it was the story of how "Eddie, through the death of Phil, was saved from being Mickey." Clearly it seemed to me that, though I had been unable at that point to delineate the steps by which this pattern progressed, I had been correct in what instinct had conceived for me. Perhaps now I hoped I might be able to uncover the exact way this theme was the essence of the play itself.

Intending to publish in this afterword what I might discover, I wrote pages and pages on the various relationships within the play, but in the end decided that their publication would be inadvisable. General thematic guidelines might be fairly suggested, but to attempt detailed instructions would be, I felt, an intrusive mistake, however much these instructions might have impressed me as appropriate.

Also, I had come in the aftermath of the production to feel that much of what we had excised from the original text had not been cut merely to contend with undue length but to alter meaning and invent intent. Though I had addressed this issue in the published text I nevertheless found that, because I had been provoked, much of what I was writing to the purpose of interpretation was in fact rebuttal, and because it was rebuttal, it was symbiotically connected to that which it challenged and to this extent, which was large, it was not free. With this realization I ended all thought of any step-by-step analysis for publication, and considered seriously, and with some relief, the complete abandonment of the idea of this afterword.

Yet the briefest contemplation of this decision put me face-to-face with my desire to make available to any interested reader the quotes I had found which had so intrigued me. To simply place them at the front of the book would run inescapably the risk of creating the impression that I had read them and then written the play according to their directions, which would not be merely a mistaken impression, but a hugely mistaken impression. For I knew without a doubt that had I read them prior to having written the play, I would not have understood them, let alone been capable of creating some dramatic, schematic demonstration of them.

And so, out of these varied circumstances and impulses, was fashioned this rather peculiar, though from my vantage point enjoyable, essay. The reader may take it as he pleases, which of course is something he hardly needs my permission or encouragement to do.

What I do feel justified, if not even obligated, to declare, however, is my sense that the play is its own expression, and by this I mean it has no "mouthpiece" character. No one in it knows what it is about. It has no character who is its spokesman. Not Eddie, and certainly not Mickey. Though it might be said that the play finally makes itself manifest through Eddie, he is not its embodiment, and he does not understand it.

Because in the end the essential core of the thing is in "accidents" and "destiny" and the idea that in some way they are the same thing. For, in all honesty, who among us would have devised the life he is living, however good or bad it might be at any given moment, when it must have its ultimate, inescapable and unforseeable end? Were we not, I thought, all making do with what we had been given, and taking credit for having accomplished far more than we had in fact determined? Because always under the little we could will and then attain there was some unknown immensity on which we stood and all utterly beyond us. As the simplest and most obvious example, is not each heartbeat again and again beyond our control? Who would ever will for himself any death or calamity? Not even the suicide in fact wills "death." For a person cannot will an event of which he is utterly ignorant. The cessation of life is not death. The willful cessation takes us into something about which we know nothing, definitively, however educated our guess, however confident our logic. At the stopping of life there will be an unknown something or nothing at all, and neither is anything with which we can claim familiarity, or over which we can claim dominion. And if the bad or undesirable was then so clearly beyond our reach, on the basis of what grandiose system of self-deception did we take credit for the good?

In other words, not only did the play have no "spokesman," but it progressed on the basis of its theme—that out of apparent accidents is hewn destiny. It consisted of scenes in which no character understood correctly the nature of the events in which he was involved, nor did anyone perceive "correctly" their consequences. Beat by beat, then, the play progressed with each character certain about the point of the event in which he was involved, and no two characters possessing the same certainty, while beneath these abundant and conflicting personal conceptions was the event whose occurrence moved them on to what would follow, where they would each be confidently mistaken again.

Finally, a word on the title. When the play was in notes, which consisted of nothing more than the first line or two, it was called "Guy's Play." When I had finished it I had a long list of titles, none of which seemed quite appropriate.

Then one day while the play was in rehearsal I was looking at a piece of prose I had been working on in which the word "hurlyburly" occurred, and I thought, "That could be it." Still, as rehearsal progressed, there was vacillation on my part regarding the title, and there was encouragement from others regarding this vacillation. Then one morning, I awoke to find myself thinking that I should look in *Macbeth* and I would find justification for the title there. I opened my favorite copy, an old maroon edition, one volume of a set that was given to me by my father and mother, having been given to them by my Dad's mother, and there it was in the first four lines, "When the hurlyburly's done, When the battle's lost and won." Certainly I had read *Macbeth* before, and certainly I knew that the word was "Shakespearean," but until that moment I had no conscious knowledge that the word was in *Macbeth* and in the first four lines. This was for me sufficient validation, however, and it became the title and almost a lot more. For as I was readying the text for publication, and fooling with quotes of one kind or another which I might include, it occurred to me that the three acts could be titled by the first lines from *Macbeth*. I had felt for a long time that the play was in many ways a trilogy, each act an entity, a self-contained action however enhanced it might be by the contents of the other acts and the reflections that might be sent back and forth between all three.

So for a time I considered naming the three acts, "When Shall We Three Meet Again?", "In Thunder, Lightning or in Rain?" and "When the Hurlyburly's Done, When the Battle's Lost and Won," but in the end decided against it.

Selected Grove Press Paperbacks

62334-7 ACKER, KATHY / Blood and Guts in High School / $7.95
62480-7 ACKER, KATHY / Great Expectations: A Novel / $6.95
62192-1 ALIFANO, ROBERTO / Twenty-four Conversations with Borges, 1980-1983 / $8.95
17458-5 ALLEN, DONALD & BUTTERICK, GEORGE F., eds. / The Postmoderns: The New American Poetry Revised 1945-1960 / $9.95
17801-7 ALLEN, DONALD M., & TALLMAN, WARREN, eds. / Poetics of the New American Poetry / $12.50
17061-X ARDEN, JOHN / Arden: Plays One (Sergeant Musgrave's Dance, The Workhouse Donkey, Armstrong's Last Goodnight) / $4.95
17657-X ARSAN, EMMANUELLE / Emmanuelle / $3.95
17213-2 ARTAUD, ANTONIN / The Theater and Its Double / $6.95
62433-5 BARASH, D. and LIPTON, J. / Stop Nuclear War! A Handbook / $7.95
62056-9 BARRY, TOM, WOOD, BETH & PREUSCH, DEB / The Other Side of Paradise: Foreign Control in the Caribbean / $9.95
17087-3 BARNES, JOHN / Evita—First Lady: A Biography of Eva Peron / $4.95
17928-5 BECKETT, SAMUEL / Company / $3.95
62489-0 BECKETT, SAMUEL / Disjecta: Miscellaneous Writings and a Dramatic Fragment, ed. Cohn, Ruby / $5.95
17208-6 BECKETT, SAMUEL / Endgame / $3.50
17953-6 BECKETT, SAMUEL / Ill Seen Ill Said / $4.95
62061-5 BECKETT, SAMUEL / Ohio Impromptu, Catastrophe, and What Where: Three Plays / $4.95
17924-2 BECKETT, SAMUEL / Rockababy and Other Short Pieces / $3.95
17299-X BECKETT, SAMUEL / Three Novels: Molloy, Malone Dies and The Unnamable / $6.95
17204-3 BECKETT, SAMUEL / Waiting for Godot / $3.50
62418-1 BERLIN, NORMAND / Eugene O'Neill / $9.95
17237-X BIELY, ANDREW / St. Petersburg / $12.50
17252-3 BIRCH, CYRIL & KEENE, DONALD, eds. / Anthology of Chinese Literature,Vvol. I: From Early Times to the 14th Century / $17.50
17766-5 BIRCH, CYRIL, ed. / Anthology of Chinese Literature, Vol. II: From the 14th Century to the Present / $12.95
62104-2 BLOCH, DOROTHY / "So the Witch Won't Eat Me," Fantasy and the Child's Fear of Infanticide / $7.95
17244-2 BORGES, JORGE LUIS / Ficciones / $6.95
17270-1 BORGES, JORGE LUIS / A Personal Anthology / $6.95

17258-2	BRECHT, BERTOLT / The Caucasian Chalk Circle / $4.95
17109-8	BRECHT, BERTOLT / The Good Woman of Setzuan / $3.95
17112-8	BRECHT, BERTOLT / Galileo / $3.95
17065-2	BRECHT, BERTOLT / The Mother / $2.95
17106-3	BRECHT, BERTOLT / Mother Courage and Her Children / $2.95
17472-0	BRECHT, BERTOLT / Threepenny Opera / $2.45
17393-7	BRETON ANDRE / Nadja / $6.95
17439-9	BULGAKOV, MIKHAIL / The Master and Margarita / $5.95
17108-X	BURROUGHS, WILLIAM S. / Naked Lunch / $4.95
17749-5	BURROUGHS, WILLIAM S. / The Soft Machine, Nova Express, The Wild Boys: Three Novels / $5.95
62488-2	CLARK, AL, ed. / The Film Year Book 1984 / $12.95
17038-5	CLEARY, THOMAS / The Original Face: An Anthology of Rinzai Zen / $4.95
17735-5	CLEVE, JOHN / The Crusader Books I and II / $4.95
17411-9	CLURMAN, HAROLD (Ed.) / Nine Plays of the Modern Theater (Waiting for Godot by Samuel Beckett, The Visit by Friedrich Durrenmatt, Tango by Slawomir Mrozek, The Caucasian Chalk Circle by Bertolt Brecht, The Balcony by Jean Genet, Rhinoceros by Eugene Ionesco, American Buffalo by David Mamet, The Birthday Party by Harold Pinter, Rosencrantz and Guildenstern Are Dead by Tom Stoppard) / $14.95
17962-5	COHN, RUBY / New American Dramatists: 1960-1980 / $7.95
17971-4	COOVER, ROBERT / Spanking the Maid / $4.95
17535-2	COWARD, NOEL / Three Plays by Noel Coward (Private Lives, Hay Fever, Blithe Spirit) / $7.95
17740-1	CRAFTS, KATHY & HAUTHER, BRENDA / How To Beat the System: The Student's Guide to Good Grades / $3.95
17219-1	CUMMINGS, E.E. / 100 Selected Poems / $3.95
17329-5	DOOLITTLE, HILDA / Selected Poems of H.D. / $8.95
17863-7	DOSS, MARGOT PATTERSON / San Francisco at Your Feet (Second Revised Edition) / $8.95
17398-8	DOYLE, RODGER, & REDDING, JAMES / The Complete Food Handbook (revised any updated edition) / $3.50
17219-1	DURAS, MARGUERITE / Four Novels: The Afternoon of Mr. Andesmas; 10:30 on a Summer Night; Moderato Cantabile; The Square) / $9.95
17246-9	DURRENMATT, FRIEDRICH / The Physicists / $6.95
17239-6	DURRENMATT, FRIEDRICH / The Visit / $4.95
17990-0	FANON, FRANZ / Black Skin, White Masks / $8.95
17327-9	FANON, FRANZ / The Wretched of the Earth / $4.95
17754-1	FAWCETT, ANTHONY / John Lennon: One Day At A Time, A Personal Biography (Revised Edition) / $8.95
17902-1	FEUERSTEIN, GEORG / The Essence of Yoga / $3.95

62455-6	FRIED, GETTLEMAN, LEVENSON & PECKENHAM, eds. / Guatemala in Rebellion: Unfinished History / $8.95
17483-6	FROMM, ERICH / The Forgotten Language / $6.95
62073-9	GARWOOD, DARRELL / Under Cover: Thirty-five Years of CIA Deception / $3.95
17222-1	GELBER, JACK / The Connection / $3.95
17390-2	GENET, JEAN / The Maids and Deathwatch: Two Plays / $8.95
17470-4	GENET, JEAN / The Miracle of the Rose / $7.95
17903-X	GENET, JEAN / Our Lady of the Flowers / $3.95
17956-0	GETTLEMAN, LACEFIELD, MENASHE, MERMELSTEIN, & RADOSH, eds. / El Salvador: Central America in the New Cold War / $9.95
17994-3	GIBBS, LOIS MARIE / Love Canal: My Story / $6.95
17648-0	GIRODIAS, MAURICE, ed. / The Olympia Reader / $5.95
17067-9	GOMBROWICZ, WITOLD / Three Novels: Ferdydurke, Pornografia and Cosmos / $12.50
17764-9	GOVER, ROBERT / One Hundred Dollar Misunderstanding / $2.95
17832-7	GREENE, GERALD and CAROLINE / SM: The Last Taboo / $2.95
62490-4	GUITAR PLAYER MAGAZINE / The Guitar Player Book (Revised and Updated Edition) $11.95
17124-1	HARRIS, FRANK / My Life and Loves / $9.95
17936-6	HARWOOD, RONALD / The Dresser / $5.95
17653-7	HAVEL, VACLAV, The Memorandum / $5.95
17022-9	HAYMAN, RONALD / How To Read A Play / $6.95
17125-X	HOCHHUTH, ROLF / The Deputy / $7.95
62115-8	HOLMES, BURTON / The Olympian Games in Athens: The First Modern Olympics, 1896 / $6.95
17241-8	HUMPHREY, DORIS / The Art of Making Dances / $9.95
17075-X	INGE, WILLIAM / Four Plays (Come Back, Little Sheba; Picnic; Bus Stop; The Dark at the Top of the Stairs) / $7.95
62199-9	IONESCO, EUGENE / Exit the King, The Killer, Macbett / $9.95
17209-4	IONESCO, EUGENE / Four Plays (The Bald Soprano, The Lesson, The Chairs, and Jack or The Submission) / $6.95
17226-4	IONESCO, EUGENE / Rhinoceros and Other Plays / $5.95
17485-2	JARRY, ALFRED / The Ubu Plays (Ubu Rex, Ubu Cuckolded, Ubu Enchained) / $9.95
62123-9	JOHNSON, CHARLES / Oxherding Tale / $6.95
62124-7	JORGENSEN, ELIZABETH WATIKINS & HENRY IRVIN / Eric Berne, Master Gamesman: A Transactional Biography / $9.95
17200-0	KEENE, DONALD, ed. / Japanese Literature: An Introduction for Western Readers-$2.25
17221-3	KEENE, DONALD, ed. / Anthology of Japanese Literature: Earliest Era to Mid-19th Century / $12.50

17278-7 KEROUAC, JACK / Dr. Sax / $5.95
17171-3 KEROUAC, JACK / Lonesome Traveler / $5.95
17287-6 KEROUAC, JACK / Mexico City Blues / $9.95
17437-2 KEROUAC, JACK / Satori in Paris / $4.95
17035-0 KERR, CARMEN / Sex for Women Who Want to Have Fun and
         Loving Relationships With Equals / $9.95
17981-1 KINGSLEY, PHILIP / The Complete Hair Book: The Ultimate
         Guide to Your Hair's Health and Beauty / $10.95
62424-6 LAWRENCE, D.H. / Lady Chatterley's Lover / $3.95
17178-0 LESTER, JULIUS / Black Folktales / $4.95
17481-X LEWIS, MATTHEW / The Monk / $8.95
17391-0 LINSSEN, ROBERT / Living Zen / $12.50
17114-4 MALCOLM X (Breitman., ed.) / Malcolm X Speaks / $5.95
17023-7 MALRAUX, ANDRE/The Conquerors/$3.95
17068-7 MALRAUX, ANDRE/Lazarus/$2.95
17093-8 MALRAUX, ANDRE / Man's Hope / $12.50
17016-4 MAMET, DAVID / American Buffalo / $4.95
62049-6 MAMET, DAVID / Glengarry Glenn Ross / $6.95
17040-7 MAMET, DAVID / A Life in the Theatre / $6.95
17043-1 MAMET, DAVID / Sexual Perversity in Chicago & The Duck
         Variations / $6.95
17471-2 MILLER, HENRY / Black Spring / $4.95
17760-6 MILLER, HENRY / Tropic of Cancer / $4.95
17295-7 MILLER, HENRY / Tropic of Capricorn / $3.95
17933-1 MROZEK, SLAWOMIR / Three Plays: Striptease, Tango,
         Vatzlav / $12.50
17869-6 NERUDA, PABLO / Five Decades: Poems 1925-1970.
         bilingual ed. / $12.50
62243-X NICOSIA, GERALD / Memory Babe: A Critical Biography of Jack
         Kerouac
17092-X ODETS, CLIFFORD / Six Plays (Waiting for Lefty, Awake and
         Sing, Golden Boy, Rocket to the Moon, Till the Day I Die,
         Paradise Lost) / $7.95
17650-2 OE, KENZABURO / A Personal Matter / $6.95
17002-4 OE, KENZABURO / Teach Us To Outgrow Our Madness (The
         Day He Himself Shall Wipe My Tears Away; Prize Stock; Teach
         Us to Outgrow Our Madness; Aghwee The Sky Monster) / $4.95
17242-6 PAZ, OCTAVIO / The Labyrinth of Solitude / $9.95
17084-9 PINTER, HAROLD / Betrayal / $6.95
17232-9 PINTER, HAROLD / The Birthday Party & The Room / $6.95
17251-5 PINTER, HAROLD / The Homecoming / $5.95
17539-5 POMERANCE / The Elephant Man / $5.95
62013-5 PORTWOOD, DORIS / Common Sense Suicide: The Final
         Right / $8.00

17658-8	REAGE, PAULINE / The Story of O, Part II; Return to the Chateau / $3.95
62169-7	RECHY, JOHN / City of Night / $4.50
62171-9	RECHY, JOHN / Numbers / $8.95
17983-8	ROBBE-GRILLET, ALAIN / Djinn / $4.95
62423-8	ROBBE—GRILLET, ALAIN / For a New Novel: Essays on Fiction / $9.95
17119-5	ROBBE-GRILLET, ALAIN / The Voyeur / 4.95
17490-9	ROSSET, BARNEY, ed. / Evergreen Review Reader: 1962-1967 / $12.50
62498-X	ROSSET, PETER and VANDERMEER, JOHN / The Nicaragua Reader: Documents of a Revolution under Fire / $9.95
17446-1	RULFO, JUAN / Pedro Paramo / $3.95
17123-3	SADE, MARQUIS DE / Justine; Philosophy in the Bedroom; Eugenie de Franval; and Other Writings / $12.50
17979-X	SANTINI, ROSEMARIE / The Secret Fire: How Women Live Their Sexual Fantasies / $3.95
62495-5	SCHEFFLER, LINDA / Help Thy Neighbor: How Counseling Works and When It Doesn't / $7.95
62438-6	SCHNEEBAUM, TOBIAS / Keep the River on Your Right / $12.50
17467-4	SELBY, HUBERT, JR. / Last Exit to Brooklyn / $3.95
17948-X	SHAWN, WALLACE, & GREGORY, ANDRE / My Dinner with Andre / $6.95
62496-3	SIEGAL AND SIEGAL / AIDS: The Medical Mystery / $7.95
17887-4	SINGH, KHUSHWANT / Train to Pakistan / $4.50
17797-5	SNOW, EDGAR / Red Star Over China / $9.95
17939-0	SRI NISARGADATA MAHARAJ / Seeds of Consciousness / $9.95
17923-4	STEINER, CLAUDE / Healing Alcoholism / $6.95
17926-9	STEINER, CLAUDE / The Other Side of Power / $6.95
17866-1	STOPPARD, TOM / Jumpers / $4.95
17260-4	STOPPARD, TOM / Rosencrantz and Guildenstern Are Dead / $3.95
17884-X	STOPPARD, TOM / Travesties / $3.95
17912-9	STRYK, LUCIEN, ed. / The Crane's Bill: Zen Poems of China and Japan / $4.95
17474-7	SUZUKI, D.T. / Introduction to Zen Buddhism / $3.95
17224-8	SUZUKI, D.T. / Manual of Zen Buddhism / $7.95
17599-9	THELWELL, MICHAEL / The Harder They Come: A Novel about Jamaica / $7.95
17969-2	TOOLE, JOHN KENNEDY / A Confederacy of Dunces / $4.50
17403-8	TROCCHI, ALEXANDER / Cain's Book / $3.50
62168-9	TUTUOLA, AMOS / The Palm-Wine Drinkard / $4.50
62189-1	UNGERER, TOMI / Far Out Isn't Far Enough (Illus.) / $12.95
17560-3	VITHOULKAS, GEORGE / The Science of Homeopathy / $12.50

17331-7 WALEY, ARTHUR / The Book of Songs / $9.95
17211-6 WALEY, ARTHUR / Monkey / $8.95
17207-8 WALEY, ARTHUR / The Way and Its Power: A Study of the Tao
         Te Ching and Its Place in Chinese Thought / $8.95
17418-6 WATTS, ALAN W. / The Spirit of Zen / $3.95
62031-3 WORTH, KATHERINE / Oscar Wilde / $8.95
17739-8 WYCKOFF, HOGIE / Solving Problems Together / $7.95

GROVE PRESS, INC., 196 West Houston St., New York, N.Y. 10014

Selected Grove Press Theater Paperbacks

17061-X ARDEN, JOHN / Plays: One (Serjeant Musgrave's Dance; The Workhouse Donkey; Armstrong's Last Goodnight) / $4.95

17083-0 AYCKBOURN, ALAN / Absurd Person Singular, Absent Friends, Bedroom Farce: Three Plays / $3.95

17208-6 BECKETT, SAMUEL / Endgame / $3.50

17233-7 BECKETT, SAMUEL / Happy Days / $4.95

62061-5 BECKETT, SAMUEL / Ohio Impromptu, Catastrophe, and What Where: Three Plays / $4.95

17204-3 BECKETT, SAMUEL / Waiting for Godot / $3.50

17112-8 BRECHT, BERTOLT / Galileo / $3.50

17472-0 BRECHT, BERTOLT / The Threepenny Opera / $2.45

17411-9 CLURMAN, HAROLD / Nine Plays of the Modern Theater (Waiting for Godot by Samuel Beckett; The Visit by Friedrich Durrenmatt; Tango by Slawomir Mrozek; The Caucasian Chalk Circle by Bertolt Brecht; The Balcony by Jean Genet; Rhinoceros by Eugene Ionesco; American Buffalo by David Mamet; The Birthday Party by Harold Pinter; and Rosencrantz and Guildenstern Are Dead by Tom Stoppard) / $11.95

17535-2 COWARD, NOEL / Three Plays (Private Lives; Hay Fever; Blithe Spirit) / $7.95

17239-6 DURRENMATT, FRIEDRICH / The Visit / $4.95

17214-0 GENET, JEAN / The Balcony / $7.95

17390-2 GENET, JEAN / The Maids and Deathwatch: Two Plays / $6.95

17022-9 HAYMAN, RONALD / How to Read a Play / $6.95

17075-X INGE, WILLIAM / Four Plays (Come Back, Little Sheba; Picnic; Bus Stop; The Dark at the Top of the Stairs) / $7.95

62199-9 IONESCO, EUGENE / Exit the King, The Killer and Macbett / $9.95

17209-4 IONESCO, EUGENE / Four Plays (The Bald Soprano; The Lesson; The Chairs; Jack or The Submission) $6.95

17226-4 IONESCO, EUGENE / Rhinoceros and Other Plays (The Leader; The Future Is in Eggs; or It Takes All Sorts to Make a World) / $5.95

17485-2 JARRY, ALFRED / The Ubu Plays (Ubu Rex; Ubu Cuckolded; Ubu Enchained) / $9.95

17744-4 KAUFMAN, GEORGE and HART, MOSS / Three Plays (Once in a Lifetime; You Can't Take It With You; The Man Who Came to Dinner) / $6.95

17016-4 MAMET, DAVID / American Buffalo / $4.95

62049-6 MAMET, DAVID / Glengarry Glen Ross / $6.95

17040-7 MAMET, DAVID / A Life in the Theatre / $6.95

17043-1 MAMET, DAVID / Sexual Perversity in Chicago and The Duck Variations / $5.95

17264-7 MROZEK, SLAWOMIR / Tango / $3.95

17092-X ODETS, CLIFFORD / Six Plays (Waiting for Lefty; Awake and Sing; Golden Boy; Rocket to the Moon; Till the Day I Die; Paradise Lost) / $7.95

17001-6 ORTON, JOE / The Complete Plays (The Ruffian on the Stair; The Good and Faithful Servant; The Erpingham Camp; Funeral Games; Loot; What the Butler Saw; Entertaining Mr. Sloan) / $6.95

17084-9 PINTER, HAROLD / Betrayal / $3.95

17019-9 PINTER, HAROLD / Complete Works: One (The Birthday Party; The Room; The Dumb Waiter; A Slight Ache; A Night Out; The Black and White; The Examination) $6.95

17020-2 PINTER, HAROLD / Complete Works: Two (The Caretaker; Night School; The Dwarfs; The Collection; The Lover; Five Revue Sketches) / $6.95

17051-2 PINTER, HAROLD / Complete Works: Three (The Homecoming; Landscape; Silence; The Basement; Six Revue Sketches; Tea party [play]; Tea Party [short story]; Mac) / $6.95

17950-1 PINTER, HAROLD / Complete Works: Four (Old Times; No Man's Land; Betrayal; Monologue; Family Voices) / $5.95

17251-5 PINTER, HAROLD / The Homecoming / $5.95

17885-8 PINTER, HAROLD / No Man's Land / $3.95

17539-5 POMERANCE, BERNARD / The Elephant Man / $5.95

17743-6 RATTIGAN, TERENCE / Plays: One (French Without Tears; The Winslow Boy; Harlequinade; The Browning Version) / $5.95

62040-2 SETO, JUDITH ROBERTS / The Young Actor's Workbook / $8.95

17948-X SHAWN, WALLACE and GREGORY, ANDRE / My Dinner with André / $6.95

17260-4 STOPPARD, TOM / Rosencrantz and Guildenstern Are Dead / $3.95

17884-X STOPPARD, TOM / Travesties / $3.95

17206-X WALEY, ARTHUR, tr. and ed. / The Nō Plays of Japan / $7.95

Available from your local bookstore, or directly from Grove Press. (Add $1.00 postage and handling for the first book and 50¢ for each additional book.)

GROVE PRESS, INC., 196 West Houston St., New York, N.Y. 10014